(ex•ploring) SERIES

1. To investigate in a systematic way: examine. 2. To search
into or range over for the purpose of discovery.

Microsoft® Office

Access 2007

VOLUME 1

Robert T. Grauer

Maurie Wigman Lockley | Keith Mulbery

PEARSON

Prentice
Hall

Upper Saddle River
New Jersey 07458

Library of Congress Cataloging-in-Publication Data
Grauer, Robert T., 1945-
  Microsoft Office Access 2007 / Robert T. Grauer.
    p. cm.
  Includes index.
  ISBN-13: 978-0-13-225212-6
  ISBN-10: 0-13-225212-0
1. Microsoft Access. 2. Database management. I. Title.
  QA76.9.D3G719595 2007
  005.75'65—dc22

                              2007015468

Vice President and Publisher: Natalie E. Anderson
Associate VP/ Executive Acquisitions Editor, Print: Stephanie Wall
Executive Acquisitions Editor, Media: Richard Keaveny
Sr. Acquisitions Editor: Melissa Sabella
Product Development Manager: Eileen Bien Calabro
Sr. Editorial Project Manager: Jennifer Frew
Sr. Editorial Project Manager/Development: Eileen Clark
Editorial Project Manager/Assistant Editor: Jenelle J. Woodrup
Market Development Editor: Claire Hunter
Editorial Assistants: Rebecca Knauer, Lora Cimiluca
Executive Producer: Lisa Strite
Content Development Manager: Cathi Profitko
Project Manager, Media: Alana Meyers
Director of Marketing: Margaret Waples
Sr. Marketing Manager: Scott Davidson
Sr. Sales Associate: Rebecca Scott
Sr. Managing Editor: Cynthia Zonneveld
Associate Managing Editor: Camille Trentacoste
Production Project Manager: Lynne Breitfeller
Senior Operations Supervisor: Nick Sklitsis
Production/Editorial Assistant: Sandra K. Bernales
Design Director: Maria Lange
Art Director/Interior and Cover Design: Blair Brown
Cover Illustration/Photo: Courtesy of Getty Images/Laurent Hamels
Composition: GGS Book Services
Project Management: GGS Book Services
Project Manager: Kevin Bradley
Production Editors: Blair Woodcock and Andrea Shearer
Cover Printer: Phoenix Color
Printer/Binder: Banta/Menasha

1 0 9 8 7 6 5 4 3 2
ISBN-13: 978-0-13-225212-6
ISBN-10: 0-13-225212-0

Dedications

To Marion—my wife, my lover, and my best friend.

Robert Grauer

I would like to express appreciation for my family's patience and support as I have worked on this project. Elizabeth, Aaron, and James were extraordinarily understanding and cooperative about letting me work. I need to acknowledge Dan Bullard for his continuing source of motivation and inspiration. Most of all, I need to thank my best friend and husband, Jim, for always believing in me.

Maurie Wigman Lockley

I would like to dedicate this book to my family and close friends who provided a strong community of emotional support as I completed my doctorate program.

Keith Mulbery

About the Authors

Dr. Robert T. Grauer

Dr. Robert T. Grauer is an Associate Professor in the Department of Computer Information Systems at the University of Miami, where he has been honored with the Outstanding Teacher Award in the School of Business. He is the vision behind the Exploring Series, which is about to sell its 3 millionth copy.

Dr. Grauer has written more than 50 books on programming and information systems. His work has been translated into three foreign languages and is used in all aspects of higher education at both national and international levels.

Dr. Grauer also has been a consultant to several major corporations including IBM and American Express. He received his Ph.D. in operations research in 1972 from the Polytechnic Institute of Brooklyn.

Maurie Wigman Lockley

Maurie Wigman Lockley teaches desktop applications and management information systems classes at the University of North Carolina Greensboro. She has been an instructor there since 1990.

She lives in a tiny piedmont North Carolina town with her husband, daughter, and two preschool-aged grandsons. She spends her free time playing with the boys, reading, camping, playing computer games, and singing. She serves on several not-for-profit boards and is active at her church.

Dr. Keith Mulbery

Dr. Keith Mulbery is an Associate Professor in the Information Systems and Technology Department at Utah Valley State College, where he teaches computer applications, programming, and MIS classes. He has written more than 15 software textbooks and business communication test banks. In January 2001, he received the Utah Valley State College Board of Trustees Award of Excellence for authoring *MOUS Essentials Word 2000*. In addition to his series editor and authoring experience, he also served as a developmental editor on two word processing textbooks.

He received his B.S. and M.Ed. (majoring in Business Education) from Southwestern Oklahoma State University and earned his Ph.D. in Education with an emphasis in Business Information Systems at Utah State University in 2006. His dissertation topic was computer-assisted instruction using TAIT to supplement traditional instruction in basic computer proficiency courses.

Brief Contents

Contents

Acknowledgments

The success of the Exploring series is attributed to contributions from numerous individuals. First and foremost, our heartfelt appreciation to Melissa Sabella, senior acquisitions editor, for providing new leadership and direction to capitalize on the strength and tradition of the Exploring series while implementing innovative ideas into the Exploring Office 2007 edition. Scott Davidson, senior marketing manager, was an invaluable addition to the team who believes in the mission of this series passionately and did an amazing job communicating its message.

During the first few months of the project, Eileen Clark, senior editorial project manager, kept the team focused on the vision, pedagogy, and voice that has been the driving force behind the success of the Exploring series. Claire Hunter, market development editor, facilitated communication between the editorial team and the reviewers to ensure that this edition meets the changing needs of computer professors and students at the collegiate level. Keith Mulbery gave up many nights and weekends (including Thanksgiving) to jump in and help out with anything that was asked of him while also managing to complete his PhD.

Jen Frew, editorial project manager, masterfully managed the flow of manuscript files among the authors, editorial team, and production to ensure timely publication of the series. Laura Town, developmental editor, provided an objective perspective in reviewing the content and organization of selected chapters. Jenelle Woodrup, editorial project manager, provided valuable assistance in communication among team members and keeping the files moving into production. Eileen Calabro, product development manager, facilitated communication among the editorial team, authors, and production during a transitional stage. Doug Bell and the whole team at GGS worked through software delays, style changes and anything else we threw at them to bring the whole thing together. Art director Blair Brown's conversations with students and professors across the country yielded a design that addressed the realities of today's students with function and style.

A special thanks to the following for the use of their work in the PowerPoint section of the text: Cameron Martin, Ph.D., Assistant to the President, Utah Valley State College, for the use of the Institutional Policies and Procedures Approval Process flowchart; Nick Finner, Paralegal Studies, Utah Valley State College, for the use of his research relating to the elderly population residing in the prisons of Utah; Ryan Phillips, Xeric Landscape and Design (XericUtah.com), for sharing Xeric's concepts for creating beautiful, drought-tolerant landscapes and for the photographs illustrating these concepts; Jo Porter, Photographer, Mapleton, Utah, for allowing the use of her beautiful engagement and wedding photographs; and David and Ali Valeti for the photographs of their baby and their family.

The following organizations and individuals generously provided data and structure from their organizational databases: Replacements, Ltd., Shweta Ponnappa, JC Raulston Arboretum at North Carolina State University, and Valerie Tyson. We deeply appreciate the ability to give students a feel for "real" data.

The new members of the Exploring author team would like to especially thank Bob Grauer for his vision in developing Exploring and his leadership in creating this highly successful series.

Maryann Barber would like to thank Bob Grauer for a wonderful collaboration and providing the opportunities through which so much of her life has changed.

The Exploring team would like to especially thank the following instructors who drew on their experience in the classroom and their software expertise to give us daily advice on how to improve this book. Their impact can be seen on every page:

Barbara Stover, Marion Technical College

Bob McCloud, Sacred Heart University

Cassie Georgetti, Florida Technical College

Dana Johnson, North Dakota State University

Jackie Lamoureux, Central New Mexico Community College

Jim Pepe, Bentley College

Judy Brown, The University of Memphis

Lancie Anthony Affonso, College of Charleston

Mimi Duncan, University of Missouri – St. Louis

Minnie Proctor, Indian River Community College

Richard Albright, Goldey-Beacom College

We also want to acknowledge all the reviewers of the Exploring 2007 series. Their valuable comments and constructive criticism greatly improved this edition:

Aaron Schorr
Fashion Institute of Technology

Alicia Stonesifer
La Salle University

Allen Alexander, Delaware
Tech & Community College

Amy Williams, Abraham
Baldwin Agriculture College

Annie Brown
Hawaii Community College

Barbara Cierny
Harper College

Barbara Hearn
Community College of Philadelphia

Barbara Meguro
University of Hawaii at Hilo

Bette Pitts
South Plains College

Beverly Fite
Amarillo College

Bill Wagner
Villanova

Brandi N. Guidry
University of Louisiana at Lafayette

Brian Powell
West Virginia University – Morgantown
Campus

Carl Farrell
Hawaii Pacific University

Carl Penzuil
Ithaca College

Carole Bagley;
University of St. Thomas

Catherine Hain
Central New Mexico CC

Charles Edwards
University of Texas of the Permian Basin

Christine L. Moore
College of Charleston

David Barnes
Penn State Altoona

David Childress;
Ashland Community College

David Law, Alfred
State College

Dennis Chalupa
Houston Baptist

Diane Stark
Phoenix College

Dianna Patterson
Texarkana College

Dianne Ross
University of Louisiana at Lafayette

Dr. Behrooz Saghafi
Chicago State University

Dr. Gladys Swindler
Fort Hays State University

Dr. Joe Teng
Barry University

Dr. Karen Nantz
Eastern Illinois University.

Duane D. Lintner
Amarillo College

Elizabeth Edmiston
North Carolina Central University

Erhan Uskup
Houston Community College

Fred Hills, McClellan
Community College

Gary R. Armstrong
Shippensburg University of Pennsylvania

Glenna Vanderhoof
Missouri State

Gregg Asher
Minnesota State University, Mankato

Hong K. Sung
University of Central Oklahoma

Hyekyung Clark
Central New Mexico CC

J Patrick Fenton
West Valley College

Jana Carver
Amarillo College

Jane Cheng
Bloomfield College

Janos T. Fustos
Metropolitan State College of Denver

Jeffrey A Hassett
University of Utah

Jennifer Pickle
Amarillo College

Jerry Kolata
New England Institute of Technology

Jesse Day
South Plains College

John Arehart
Longwood University

John Lee Reardon
University of Hawaii, Manoa

Joshua Mindel
San Francisco State University

Karen Wisniewski
County College of Morris

Karl Smart
Central Michigan University

Kathryn L. Hatch
University of Arizona

Krista Terry
Radford University

Laura McManamon
University of Dayton

Laura Reid
University of Western Ontario

Linda Johnsonius
Murray State University

Lori Kelley
Madison Area Technical College

Lucy Parker,
California State University, Northridge

Lynda Henrie
LDS Business College

Malia Young
Utah State University

Margie Martyn
Baldwin Wallace

Marianne Trudgeon
Fanshawe College

Marilyn Hibbert
Salt Lake Community College

Marjean Lake
LDS Business College

Mark Olaveson
Brigham Young University

Nancy Sardone
Seton Hall University

Patricia Joseph
Slippery Rock University.

Patrick Hogan
Cape Fear Community College

Paula F. Bell
Lock Haven University of Pennsylvania

Paulette Comet
Community College of Baltimore County, Catonsville

Pratap Kotala
North Dakota State University

Richard Blamer
John Carroll University

Richard Herschel
St. Joseph's University

Richard Hewer
Ferris State University

Robert Gordon
Hofstra University

Robert Marmelstein
East Stroudsburg University

Robert Stumbur
Northern Alberta Institute of Technology

Roberta I. Hollen
University of Central Oklahoma

Roland Moreira
South Plains College

Ron Murch
University of Calgary

Rory J. de Simone
University of Florida

Ruth Neal
Navarro College

Sandra M. Brown
Finger Lakes Community College

Sharon Mulroney
Mount Royal College

Stephen E. Lunce
Midwestern State University

Steve Schwarz
Raritan Valley Community College

Steven Choy
University of Calgary

Susan Byrne
St. Clair College

Thomas Setaro
Brookdale Community College

Todd McLeod
Fresno City College

Vickie Pickett
Midland College

Vipul Gupta
St Joseph's University

Vivek Shah
Texas State University - San Marcos

Wei-Lun Chuang
Utah State University

William Dorin
Indiana University Northwest

Finally, we wish to acknowledge reviewers of previous editions of the Exploring series—we wouldn't have made it to the 7th edition without you:

Alan Moltz
Naugatuck Valley Technical Community College

Alok Charturvedi
Purdue University

Antonio Vargas
El Paso Community College

Barbara Sherman
Buffalo State College

Bill Daley
University of Oregon

Bill Morse
DeVry Institute of Technology

Bonnie Homan
San Francisco State University

Carl M. Briggs
Indiana University School of Business

Carlotta Eaton
Radford University

Carolyn DiLeo
Westchester Community College

Cody Copeland
Johnson County Community College

Connie Wells
Georgia State University

Daniela Marghitu
Auburn University

David B. Meinert
Southwest Missouri State University

David Douglas
University of Arkansas

David Langley
University of Oregon

David Rinehard
Lansing Community College

David Weiner
University of San Francisco

Dean Combellick
Scottsdale Community College

Delores Pusins
Hillsborough Community College

Don Belle
Central Piedmont Community College

Douglas Cross
Clackamas Community College

Ernie Ivey
Polk Community College

Gale E. Rand
College Misericordia

Helen Stoloff
Hudson Valley Community College

Herach Safarian
College of the Canyons

Jack Zeller
Kirkwood Community College

James Franck
College of St. Scholastica

James Gips
Boston College

Jane King
Everett Community College

Janis Cox
Tri-County Technical College

Jerry Chin
Southwest Missouri State University

Jill Chapnick
Florida International University

Jim Pruitt
Central Washington University

John Lesson
University of Central Florida

John Shepherd
Duquesne University

Judith M. Fitspatrick
Gulf Coast Community College

Judith Rice
Santa Fe Community College

Judy Dolan
Palomar College

Karen Tracey
Central Connecticut State University

Kevin Pauli
University of Nebraska

Kim Montney
Kellogg Community College

Kimberly Chambers
Scottsdale Community College

Larry S. Corman
Fort Lewis College

Lynn Band
Middlesex Community College

Margaret Thomas
Ohio University

Marguerite Nedreberg
Youngstown State University

Marilyn Salas
Scottsdale Community College

Martin Crossland
Southwest Missouri State University

Mary McKenry Percival
University of Miami

Michael Hassett
Fort Hayes State University

Michael Stewardson
San Jacinto College – North

Midge Gerber
Southwestern Oklahoma State University

Mike Hearn
Community College of Philadelphia

Mike Kelly
Community College of Rhode Island

Mike Thomas
Indiana University School of Business

Paul E. Daurelle
Western Piedmont Community College

Ranette Halverson
Midwestern State University

Raymond Frost
Central Connecticut State University

Robert Spear, Prince
George's Community College

Rose M. Laird
Northern Virginia Community College

Sally Visci
Lorain County Community College

Shawna DePlonty
Sault College of Applied Arts and Technology

Stuart P. Brian
Holy Family College

Susan Fry
Boise State Universtiy

Suzanne Tomlinson
Iowa State University

Vernon Griffin
Austin Community College

Wallace John Whistance-Smith
Ryerson Polytechnic University

Walter Johnson
Community College of Philadelphia

Wanda D. Heller
Seminole Community College

We very much appreciate the following individuals for painstakingly checking every step and every explanation for technical accuracy, while dealing with an entirely new software application:

Barbara Waxer
Bill Daley
Beverly Fite
Dawn Wood
Denise Askew
Elizabeth Lockley

James Reidel
Janet Pickard
Janice Snyder
Jeremy Harris
John Griffin
Joyce Neilsen

LeeAnn Bates
Mara Zebest
Mary E. Pascarella
Michael Meyers
Sue McCrory

The Exploring Series

Exploring has been Prentice Hall's most successful Office Application series of the past 15 years. For Office 2007 Exploring has undergone the most extensive changes in its history, so that it can truly move today's student "beyond the point and click."

The goal of Exploring has always been to teach more than just the steps to accomplish a task – the series provides the theoretical foundation necessary for a student to understand when and why to apply a skill. This way, students achieve a broader understanding of Office.

Today's students are changing and Exploring has evolved with them. Prentice Hall traveled to college campuses across the country and spoke directly to students to determine how they study and prepare for class. We also spoke with hundreds of professors about the best ways to administer materials to such a diverse body of students.

Here is what we learned

Students go to college now with a different set of skills than they did 5 years ago. The new edition of Exploring moves students beyond the basics of the software at a faster pace, without sacrificing coverage of the fundamental skills that everybody needs to know. This ensures that students will be engaged from Chapter 1 to the end of the book.

Students have diverse career goals. With this in mind, we broadened the examples in the text (and the accompanying Instructor Resources) to include the health sciences, hospitality, urban planning, business and more. Exploring will be relevant to every student in the course.

Students read, prepare and study differently than they used to. Rather than reading a book cover to cover students want to easily identify what they need to know, and then learn it efficiently. We have added key features that will bring students into the content and make the text easy to use such as objective mapping, pull quotes, and key terms in the margins.

Moving students beyond the point and click

All of these additions mean students will be more engaged, achieve a higher level of understanding, and successfully complete this course. In addition to the experience and expertise of the series creator and author Robert T. Grauer we have assembled a tremendously talented team of supporting authors to assist with this critical revision. Each of them is equally dedicated to the Exploring mission of **moving students beyond the point and click.**

Key Features of the Office 2007 revision include

- **New** **Office Fundamentals Chapter** efficiently covers skills common among all applications like save, print, and bold to avoid repetition in each Office application's first chapter, along with coverage of problem solving skills to prepare students to apply what they learn in any situation.

- **New** **Moving Beyond the Basics** introduces advanced skills earlier because students are learning basic skills faster.

- **White Pages/Yellow Pages clearly** distinguish the theory (white pages) from the skills covered in the Hands-On exercises (yellow pages) so students always know what they are supposed to be doing.

- **New** **Objective Mapping** enables students to skip the skills and concepts they know, and quickly find those they don't, by scanning the chapter opener page for the page numbers of the material they need.

- **New** **Pull Quotes** entice students into the theory by highlighting the most interesting points.

- **New** **Conceptual Animations** connect the theory with the skills, by illustrating tough to understand concepts with interactive multimedia

- **New** **More End of Chapter Exercises** offer instructors more options for assessment. Each chapter has approximately 12–15 exercises ranging from Multiple Choice questions to open-ended projects.

- **New** **More Levels of End of Chapter Exercises,** including new Mid-Level Exercises tell students what to do, but not how to do it, and Capstone Exercises cover all of the skills within each chapter.

- **New** **Mini Cases with Rubrics** are open ended exercises that guide both instructors and students to a solution with a specific rubric for each mini case.

Instructor and Student Resources

Instructor Chapter Reference Cards

A four page color card for every chapter that includes a:

- *Concept Summary* that outlines the KEY objectives to cover in class with tips on where students get stuck as well as how to get them un-stuck. It helps bridge the gap between the instructor and student when discussing more difficult topics.

- *Case Study Lecture Demonstration Document* which provides instructors with a lecture sample based on the chapter opening case that will guide students to critically use the skills covered in the chapter, with examples of other ways the skills can be applied.

The Enhanced Instructor's Resource Center on CD-ROM includes:

- **Additional Capstone Production Tests** allow instructors to assess all the skills in a chapter with a single project.

- **Mini Case Rubrics** in Microsoft® Word format enable instructors to customize the assignment for their class.

- **PowerPoint® Presentations** for each chapter with notes included for online students

- **Lesson Plans** that provide a detailed blueprint for an instructor to achieve chapter learning objectives and outcomes.

- **Student Data Files**

- **Annotated Solution Files**

- **Complete Test Bank**

- **Test Gen Software with QuizMaster**

TestGen is a test generator program that lets you view and easily edit testbank questions, transfer them to tests, and print in a variety of formats suitable to your teaching situation. The program also offers many options for organizing and displaying testbanks and tests. A random number test generator enables you to create multiple versions of an exam.

QuizMaster, also included in this package, allows students to take tests created with TestGen on a local area network. The QuizMaster Utility built into TestGen lets instructors view student records and print a variety of reports. Building tests is easy with Test-Gen, and exams can be easily uploaded into WebCT, BlackBoard, and CourseCompass.

Prentice Hall's Companion Web Site

www.prenhall.com/exploring offers expanded IT resources and downloadable supplements. This site also includes an online study guide for student self-study.

Online Course Cartridges

Flexible, robust and customizable content is available for all major online course platforms that include everything instructors need in one place.
www.prenhall.com/webct
www.prenhall.com/blackboard
www.coursecompass.com

myitlab for Microsoft Office 2007, is a solution designed by professors that allows you to easily deliver Office courses with defensible assessment and outcomes-based training.

The new *Exploring Office 2007* System will seamlessly integrate online assessment and training with the new my**it**lab for Microsoft Office 2007!

Integrated Assessment and Training

To fully integrate the new my**it**lab into the *Exploring Office 2007* System we built my**it**lab assessment and training directly from the *Exploring* instructional content. No longer is the technology just mapped to your textbook.

This 1:1 content relationship between the *Exploring* text and my**it**lab means that your online assessment and training will work with your textbook to move your students beyond the point and click.

Advanced Reporting

With my**it**lab you will get advanced reporting capabilities including a detailed student click stream. This ability to see exactly what actions your students took on a test, click-by-click, provides you with true defensible grading.

In addition, myitlab for Office 2007 will feature. . .

Project-based assessment: Test students on Exploring projects, or break down assignments into individual Office application skills.

Outcomes-based training: Students train on what they don't know without having to relearn skills they already know.

Optimal performance and uptime: Provided by a world-class hosting environment.

Dedicated student and instructor support: Professional tech support is available by phone and email when you need it.

No installation required! my**it**lab runs entirely from the Web.

And much more!

www.prenhall.com/myitlab

Office Fundamentals Chapter

efficiently covers skills common among all applications like save, print, and bold to avoid repetition in each 1st application chapter.

chapter 1 | Office Fundamentals

Using Word, Excel, Access, and PowerPoint

 bjectives

After you read this chapter you will be able to:

1. Identify common interface components (**page 4**).
2. Use Office 2007 Help (**page 10**).
3. Open a file (**page 18**).
4. Save a file (**page 21**).
5. Print a document (**page 24**).
6. Select text to edit (**page 31**).
7. Insert text and change to the Overtype mode (**page 32**).
8. Move and copy text (**page 34**).
9. Find, replace, and go to text (**page 36**).
10. Use the Undo and Redo commands (**page 39**).
11. Use language tools (**page 39**).
12. Apply font attributes (**page 43**).
13. Copy formats with the Format Painter (**page 47**).

Hands-On Exercises

Exercises	Skills Covered
1. IDENTIFYING PROGRAM INTERFACE COMPONENTS AND USING HELP (page 12)	• Use PowerPoint's Office Button, Get Help in a Dialog Box, and Use the Zoom Slider • Use Excel's Ribbon, Get Help from an Enhanced ScreenTip, and Use the Zoom Dialog Box • Search Help in Access • Use Word's Status Bar • Search Help and Print a Help Topic
2. PERFORMING UNIVERSAL TASKS (page 28) **Open:** chap1_ho2_sample.docx **Save as:** chap1_ho2_solution.docx	• Open a File and Save it with a Different Name • Use Print Preview and Select Options • Print a Document
3. PERFORMING BASIC TASKS (page 48) **Open:** chap1_ho3_internet_docx **Save as:** chap_ho3_internet_solution.docx	• Cut, Copy, Paste, and Undo • Find and Replace Text • Check Spelling • Choose Synonyms and Use Thesaurus • Use the Research Tool • Apply Font Attributes • Use Format Painter

Microsoft Office 2007 Software Office Fundamentals

1

chapter 3 | **Access**

Customize, Analyze, and Summarize Query Data

Creating and Using Queries to Make Decisions

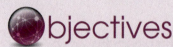bjectives

After you read this chapter you will be able to:

1. Understand the order of precedence (**page 679**).
2. Create a calculated field in a query (**page 679**).
3. Create expressions with the Expression Builder (**page 679**).
4. Create and edit Access functions (**page 690**).
5. Perform date arithmetic (**page 694**).
6. Create and work with data aggregates (**page 704**).

Hands-On Exercises

Exercises	Skills Covered
1. CALCULATED QUERY FIELDS (PAGE 683) **Open:** chap3_ho1-3_realestate.accdb **Save:** chap3_ho1-3_realestate_solution.accdb **Back up as:** chap3_ho1_realestate_solution.accdb	• Copy a Database and Start the Query • Select the Fields, Save, and Open the Query • Create a Calculated Field and Run the Query • Verify the Calculated Results • Recover from a Common Error
2. EXPRESSION BUILDER, FUNCTIONS, AND DATE ARITHMETIC (page 695) **Open:** chap3_ho1-3_realestate.accdb (from Exercise 1) **Save:** chap3_ho1-3_realestate_solution.accdb (additional modifications) **Back up as:** chap3_ho2_realestate_solution.accdb	• Create a Select Query • Use the Expression Builder • Create Calculations Using Input Stored in a Different Query or Table • Edit Expressions Using the Expression Builder • Use Functions • Work with Date Arithmetic
3. DATA AGGREGATES (page 707) **Open:** chap3_ho1-3_realestate.accdb (from Exercise 2) **Save:** chap3_ho1-3_realestate_solution.accdb (additional modifications)	• Add a Total Row • Create a Totals Query Based on a Select Query • Add Fields to the Design Grid • Add Grouping Options and Specify Summary Statistics

Objective Mapping

allows students to skip the skills and concepts they know and quickly find those they don't by scanning the chapter opening page for the page numbers of the material they need.

Case Study

begins each chapter to provide an effective overview of what students can accomplish by completing the chapter.

CASE STUDY

West Transylvania College Athletic Department

The athletic department of West Transylvania College has reached a fork in the road. A significant alumni contingent insists that the college upgrade its athletic program from NCAA Division II to Division I. This process will involve adding sports, funding athletic scholarships, expanding staff, and coordinating a variety of fundraising activities.

Tom Hunt, the athletic director, wants to determine if the funding support is available both inside and outside the college to accomplish this goal. You are helping Tom prepare the five-year projected budget based on current budget figures. The plan is to increase revenues at a rate of 10% per year for five years while handling an estimated 8% increase in expenses over the same five-year period. Tom feels that a 10% increase in revenue versus an 8% increase in expenses should make the upgrade viable. Tom wants to examine how increased alumni giving, increases in college fees, and grant monies will increase the revenue flow. The Transylvania College's Athletic Committee and its Alumni Association Board of Directors want Tom to present an analysis of funding and expenses to determine if the move to NCAA Division I is feasible. As Tom's student assistant this year, it is your responsibility to help him with special projects. Tom prepared the basic projected budget spreadsheet and has asked you to finish it for him.

Case Study

Your Assignment

- Read the chapter carefully and pay close attention to mathematical operations, formulas, and functions.
- Open *chap2_case_athletics*, which contains the partially completed, projected budget spreadsheet.
- Study the structure of the worksheet to determine what type of formulas you need to complete the financial calculations. Identify how you would perform calculations if you were using a calculator and make a list of formulas using regular language to determine if the financial goals will be met. As you read the chapter, identify formulas and functions that will help you complete the financial analysis. You will insert formulas in the revenue and expenditures sections for column C. Use appropriate cell references in formulas. Do not enter constant values within a formula; instead enter the 10% and 8% increases in an input area. Use appropriate functions for column totals in both the revenue and expenditures sections. Insert formulas for the Net Operating Margin and Net Margin rows. Copy the formulas.
- Review the spreadsheet and identify weaknesses in the formatting. Use your knowledge of good formatting design to improve the appearance of the spreadsheet so that it will be attractive to the Athletic Committee and the alumni board. You will format cells as currency with 0 decimals and widen columns as needed. Merge and center the title and use an attractive fill color. Emphasize the totals and margin rows with borders. Enter your name and current date. Create a custom footer that includes a page number and your instructor's name. Print the worksheet as displayed and again with cell formulas displayed. Save the workbook as **chap2_case_athletics_solution**.

Key Terms

are called out in the margins of the chapter so students can more effectively study definitions.

Pull Quotes

entice students into the theory by highlighting the most interesting points.

Tables

A **table** is a series of rows and columns that organize data.

A **cell** is the intersection of a row and column in a table.

> The table feature is one of the most powerful in Word and is the basis for an almost limitless variety of documents. It is very easy to create once you understand how a table works.

A *table* is a series of rows and columns that organize data effectively. The rows and columns in a table intersect to form *cells*. The table feature is one of the most powerful in Word and is an easy way to organize a series of data in a columnar list format such as employee names, inventory lists, and e-mail addresses. The Vacation Planner in Figure 3.1, for example, is actually a 4x9 table (4 columns and 9 rows). The completed table looks impressive, but it is very easy to create once you understand how a table works. In addition to the organizational benefits, tables make an excellent alignment tool. For example, you can create tables to organize data such as employee lists with phone numbers and e-mail addresses. The Exploring series uses tables to provide descriptions for various software commands. Although you can align text with tabs, you have more format control when you create a table. (See the Practice Exercises at the end of the chapter for other examples.)

Vacation Planner

Item	Number of Days	Amount per Day (est)	Total Amount
Airline Ticket			449.00
Amusement Park Tickets	4	50.00	200.00
Hotel	5	120.00	600.00
Meals	6	50.00	300.00
Rental Car	5	30.00	150.00
Souvenirs	5	20.00	100.00
TOTAL EXPECTED EXPENSES			$1799.00

Figure 3.1 The Vacation Planner

In this section, you insert a table in a document. After inserting the table, you can insert or delete columns and rows if you need to change the structure. Furthermore, you learn how to merge and split cells within the table. Finally, you change the row height and column width to accommodate data in the table.

Inserting a Table

You can create a table from the Insert tab. Click Table in the Tables group on the Insert tab to see a gallery of cells from which you select the number of columns and rows you require in the table, or you can choose the Insert Table command below the gallery to display the Insert Table dialog box and enter the table composition you prefer. When you select the table dimension from the gallery or from the Insert Table dialog box, Word creates a table structure with the number of columns and rows you specify. After you define a table, you can enter text, numbers, or graphics in individual cells. Text

White Pages/ Yellow Pages

clearly distinguishes the theory (white pages) from the skills covered in the Hands-On exercises (yellow pages) so students always know what they are supposed to be doing.

Keyword for search

Collections to be searched

Type of clips to be included in results

Search results

Link to Microsoft Clip Organizer

Link to more clips online

CIS 101 Review Session
Test #2

Monday
7pm
Glass 102

Figure 3.18 The Clip Art Task Pane

You can access the Microsoft Clip Organizer (to view the various collections) by clicking Organize clips at the bottom of the Clip Art task pane. You also can access the Clip Organizer when you are not using Word; click the Start button on the taskbar, click All Programs, Micros… Clip Organizer. Once in the Organi… ous collections, reorganize the exis… add new clips (with their associated… the bottom of the task pane in Figur… and tips for finding more relevant c…

Insert a Picture

In addition to the collection of clip … you also can insert your own pictur… ital camera attached to your compu… Word. After you save the picture to … on the Insert tab to locate and inser… opens so that you can navigate to t… insert the picture, there are many c… mands are discussed in the next sec…

Formatting a Grap…

(Remember that graphical elements should enhance a document, not overpower it.)

When you inse…
fined size. For …
very large and …
resized. Most ti…
within the d…

Step 2
Move and Resize the Clip Art Object

Refer to Figure 3.24 as you complete Step 2.

a. Click once on the clip art object to select it. Click Text Wrapping in the Arrange group on the Picture Tools Format tab to display the text wrapping options and then select Square as shown in Figure 3.24.

You must change the layout in order to move and size the object.

b. Click Position in the Arrange group, and then click More Layout Options. Click the Picture Position tab in the Advanced Layout dialog box, if necessary, then click Alignment in the *Horizontal* section. Click the Alignment drop-down arrow and select Right. Deselect the Allow overlap check box in the *Options* section. Click OK.

c. Click Crop in the Size group, then hold your mouse over the sizing handles and notice how the pointer changes to angular shapes. Click the bottom center handle and drag it up. Drag the side handles inward to remove excess space surrounding the graphical object.

d. Click the Shape Height box in the Size group and type 2.77.

Notice the width is changed automatically to retain the proportion.

e. Save the document.

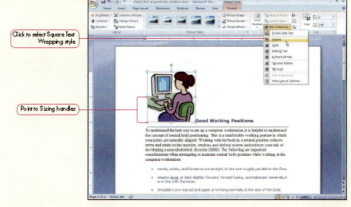

Click to select Square Text Wrapping style

Point to Sizing handles

Figure 3.24 Formatting Clip Art

Step 3
Create a WordArt Object

Refer to Figure 3.25 as you complete Step 3.

a. Press Ctrl+End to move to the end of the document. Click the Insert tab and then click WordArt in the Text group to display the WordArt gallery.

b. Click WordArt Style 28 on the bottom row of the gallery.

The Edit WordArt Text dialog box displays, as shown in Figure 3.25.

Summary

1. **Create a presentation using a template.** Using a template saves you a great deal of time and enables you to create a more professional presentation. Templates incorporate a theme, a layout, and content that can be modified. You can use templates that are installed when Microsoft Office is installed, or you can download templates from Microsoft Office Online. Microsoft is constantly adding templates to the online site for your use.

2. **Modify a template.** In addition to changing the content of a template, you can modify the structure and design. The structure is modified by changing the layout of a slide. To change the layout, drag placeholders to new locations or resize placeholders. You can even add placeholders so that elements such as logos can be included.

3. **Create a presentation in Outline view.** When you use a storyboard to determine your content, you create a basic outline. Then you can enter your presentation in Outline view, which enables you to concentrate on the content of the presentation. Using Outline view keeps you from getting buried in design issues at the cost of your content. It also saves you time because you can enter the information without having to move from placeholder to placeholder.

4. **Modify an outline structure.** Because the Outline view gives you a global view of the presentation, it helps you see the underlying structure of the presentation. You are able to see where content needs to be strengthened, or where the flow of information needs to be revised. If you find a slide with content that would be presented better in another location in the slide show, you can use the Collapse and Expand features to easily move it. By collapsing the slide content, you can drag it to a new location and then expand it. To move individual bullet points, cut and paste the bullet point or drag-and-drop it.

5. **Print an outline.** When you present, using the outline version of your slide show as a reference is a boon. No matter how well you know your information, it is easy to forget to present some information when facing an audience. While you would print speaker's notes if you have many details, you can print the outline as a quick reference. The outline can be printed in either the collapsed or the expanded form, giving you far fewer pages to shuffle in front of an audience than printing speaker's notes would.

6. **Import an outline.** You do not need to re-enter information from an outline created in Microsoft Word or another word processor. You can use the Open feature to import any outline that has been saved in a format that PowerPoint can read. In addition to a Word outline, you can use the common generic formats Rich Text Format and Plain Text Format.

7. **Add existing content to a presentation.** After you spend time creating the slides in a slide show, you may find that slides in the slide show would be appropriate in another show at a later date. Any slide you create can be reused in another presentation, thereby saving you considerable time and effort. You simply open the Reuse Slides pane, locate the slide show with the slide you need, and then click on the thumbnail of the slide to insert a copy of it in the new slide show.

8. **Examine slide show design principles.** With a basic understanding of slide show design principles you can create presentations that reflect your personality in a professional way. The goal of applying these principles is to create a slide show that focuses the audience on the message of the slide without being distracted by clutter or unreadable text.

9. **Apply and modify a design theme.** PowerPoint provides you with themes to help you create a clean, professional look for your presentation. Once a theme is applied you can modify the theme by changing the color scheme, the font scheme, the effects scheme, or the background style.

10. **Insert a header or footer.** Identifying information can be included in a header or footer. You may, for example, wish to include the group to whom you are presenting, or the location of the presentation, or a copyright notation for original work. You can apply footers to slides, handouts, and Notes pages. Headers may be applied to handouts and Notes pages.

Summary

links directly back to the objectives so students can more effectively study and locate the concepts that they need to focus on.

More End of Chapter Exercises with New Levels of Assessment

offer instructors more options for assessment. Each chapter has approximately 12-15 projects per chapter ranging from multiple choice to open-ended projects.

Practice Exercises

reinforce skills learned in the chapter with specific directions on what to do and how to do it.

New Mid-Level Exercises

assess the skills learned in the chapter by directing the students on what to do but not how to do it.

New Capstone Exercises

cover all of the skills with in each chapter without telling students how to perform the skills.

Mini Cases with Rubrics

are open ended exercises that guide both instructors and students to a solution with a specific rubric for each Mini Case.

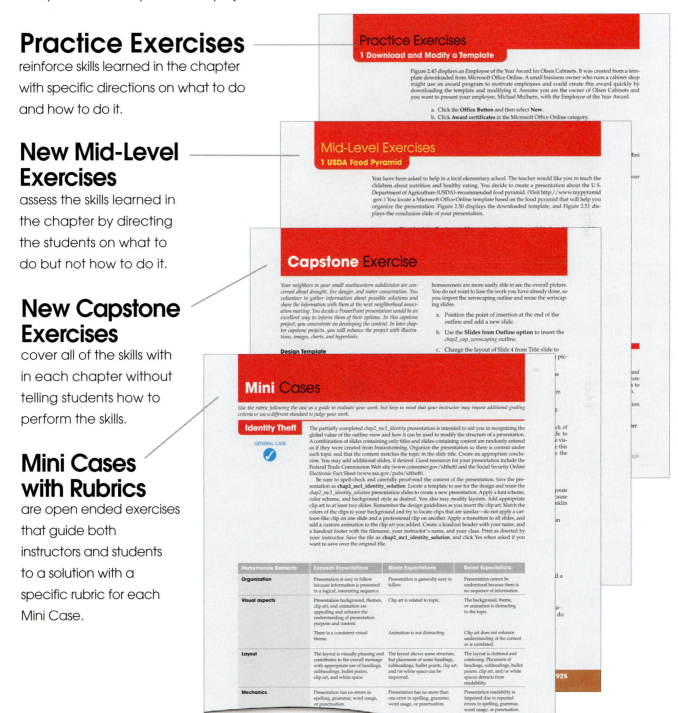

Using Word, Excel, Access, and PowerPoint

bjectives

After you read this chapter, you will be able to:

1. Identify common interface components **(page 4)**.

2. Use Office 2007 Help **(page 10)**.

3. Open a file **(page 18)**.

4. Save a file **(page 21)**.

5. Print a document **(page 24)**.

6. Select text to edit **(page 31)**.

7. Insert text and change to the Overtype mode **(page 32)**.

8. Move and copy text **(page 34)**.

9. Find, replace, and go to text **(page 36)**.

10. Use the Undo and Redo commands **(page 39)**.

11. Use language tools **(page 39)**.

12. Apply font attributes **(page 43)**.

13. Copy formats with the Format Painter **(page 47)**.

Hands-On Exercises

Exercises	Skills Covered
1. IDENTIFYING PROGRAM INTERFACE COMPONENTS AND USING HELP (page 12)	• Use PowerPoint's Office Button, Get Help in a Dialog Box, and Use the Zoom Slider • Use Excel's Ribbon, Get Help from an Enhanced ScreenTip, and Use the Zoom Dialog Box • Search Help in Access • Use Word's Status Bar • Search Help and Print a Help Topic
2. PERFORMING UNIVERSAL TASKS (page 28) **Open:** chap1_ho2_sample.docx **Save as:** chap1_ho2_solution.docx	• Open a File and Save it with a Different Name • Use Print Preview and Select Options • Print a Document
3. PERFORMING BASIC TASKS (page 48) **Open:** chap1_ho3_internet_docx **Save as:** chap_ho3_internet_solution.docx	• Cut, Copy, Paste, and Undo • Find and Replace Text • Check Spelling • Choose Synonyms and Use Thesaurus • Use the Research Tool • Apply Font Attributes • Use Format Painter

CASE STUDY
Color Theory Design

Natalie Trevino's first job after finishing her interior design degree is with Color Theory Design of San Diego. Her new supervisor has asked her to review a letter written to an important client and to make any changes or corrections she thinks will improve it. Even though Natalie has used word processing software in the past, she is unfamiliar with Microsoft Office 2007. She needs to get up to speed with Word 2007 so that she can open the letter, edit the content, format the appearance, re-save the file, and print the client letter. Natalie wants to successfully complete this important first task, plus she wants to become familiar with all of Office 2007 because she realizes that her new employer, CTD, makes extensive use of all the Office products.

Case Study

In addition, Natalie needs to improve the appearance of an Excel workbook by applying font attributes, correcting spelling errors, changing the zoom magnification, and printing the worksheet. Finally, Natalie needs to modify a short PowerPoint presentation that features supplemental design information for CTD's important client.

Your Assignment

- Read the chapter and open the existing client letter, *chap1_case_design*.
- Edit the letter by inserting and overtyping text and moving existing text to improve the letter's readability.
- Find and replace text that you want to update.
- Check the spelling and improve the vocabulary by using the thesaurus.
- Modify the letter's appearance by applying font attributes.
- Save the file as **chap1_case_design_solution**, print preview, and print a copy of the letter.
- Open the *chap1_case_bid* workbook in Excel, apply bold and blue font color to the column headings, spell-check the worksheet, change the zoom to 125%, print preview, and print the workbook. Save the workbook as **chap1_case_bid_solution**.
- Open the *chap1_case_design* presentation in PowerPoint, spell-check the presentation, format text, and save it as **chap1_case_design_solution**.

Microsoft Office 2007 Software

(Which software application should you choose? You have to start with an analysis of the output required.)

Microsoft Office 2007 is composed of several software applications, of which the primary components are Word, Excel, PowerPoint, and Access. These programs are powerful tools that can be used to increase productivity in creating, editing, saving, and printing files. Each program is a specialized and sophisticated program, so it is necessary to use the correct one to successfully complete a task, much like using the correct tool in the physical world. For example, you use a hammer, not a screwdriver, to pound a nail into the wall. Using the correct tool gets the job done correctly and efficiently the first time; using the wrong tool may require redoing the task, thus wasting time. Likewise, you should use the most appropriate software application to create and work with computer data.

Choosing the appropriate application to use in a situation seems easy to the beginner. If you need to create a letter, you type the letter in Word. However, as situations increase in complexity, so does the need to think through using each application. For example, you can create an address book of names and addresses in Word to create form letters; you can create an address list in Excel and then use spreadsheet commands to manipulate the data; further, you can store addresses in an Access database table and then use database capabilities to manipulate the data. Which software application should you choose? You have to start with an analysis of the output required. If you only want a form letter as the final product, then you might use Word; however, if you want to spot customer trends with the data and provide detailed reports, you would use Access. Table 1.1 describes the main characteristics of the four primary programs in Microsoft Office 2007 to help you decide which program to use for particular tasks.

Table 1.1 Office Products

Office 2007 Product	Application Characteristics
Word 2007	*Word processing software* is used with text to create, edit, and format documents such as letters, memos, reports, brochures, resumes, and flyers.
Excel 2007	*Spreadsheet software* is used to store quantitative data and to perform accurate and rapid calculations with results ranging from simple budgets to financial analyses and statistical analyses.
PowerPoint 2007	*Presentation graphics software* is used to create slide shows for presentation by a speaker, to be published as part of a Web site, or to run as a stand-alone application on a computer kiosk.
Access 2007	*Relational database software* is used to store data and convert it into information. Database software is used primarily for decision-making by businesses that compile data from multiple records stored in tables to produce informative reports.

Word processing software is used primarily with text to create, edit, and format documents.

Spreadsheet software is used primarily with numbers to create worksheets.

Presentation graphics software is used primarily to create electronic slide shows.

Relational database software is used to store data and convert it into information.

In this section, you explore the common interface among the programs. You learn the names of the interface elements. In addition, you learn how to use Help to get assistance in using the software.

Identifying Common Interface Components

A ***user interface*** is the meeting point between computer software and the person using it.

A ***user interface*** is the meeting point between computer software and the person using it and provides the means for a person to communicate with a software program. Word, Excel, PowerPoint, and Access share the overall Microsoft Office 2007 interface. This interface is made up of three main sections of the screen display shown in Figure 1.1.

Office Button, Quick Access Toolbar, and title bar

Ribbon

Status bar

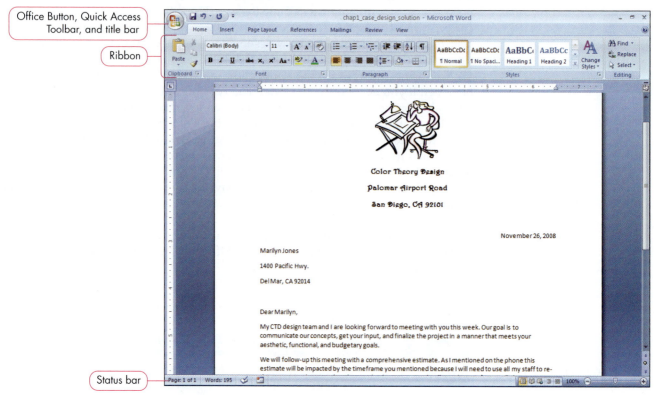

Figure 1.1   Office 2007 Interface

Use the Office Button and Quick Access Toolbar

The first section of the Office 2007 interface contains three distinct items: the Microsoft Office Button (referred to as Office Button in the Exploring series), Quick Access Toolbar, and the title bar. These three items are located at the top of the interface for quick access and reference. The following paragraphs explain each item.

Click the ***Office Button*** to display the Office menu.

The ***Office menu*** contains commands that work with an entire file or with the program.

The ***Office Button*** is an icon that, when clicked, displays the ***Office menu***, a list of commands that you can perform on the entire file or for the specific Office program. For example, when you want to perform a task that involves the entire document, such as saving, printing, or sharing a file with others, you use the commands on the Office menu. You also use the Office menu commands to work with the entire program, such as customizing program settings or exiting from the program. Some commands on the Office menu perform a default action when you click them, such as Save—the file open in the active window is saved. However, other commands open a submenu when you point to or click the command. Figure 1.2 displays the Office menu in Access 2007.

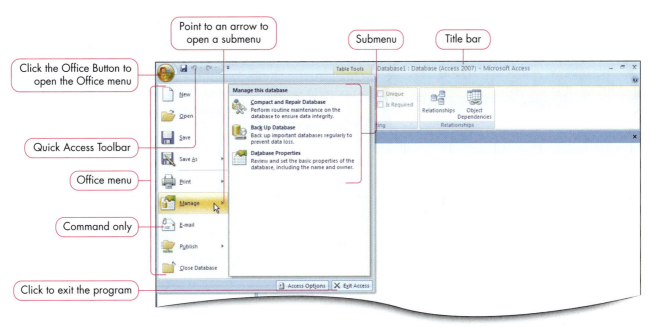

Figure 1.2 Access Office Menu

TIP Displaying the Office Menu from the Keyboard

If you prefer to use a keyboard shortcut to display the Office menu instead of clicking the Office Button, press Alt+F.

The ***Quick Access Toolbar*** contains buttons for frequently used commands.

The second item at the top of the window is the ***Quick Access Toolbar***, which contains buttons for frequently used commands, such as saving a file or undoing an action. This toolbar keeps buttons for common tasks on the screen at all times, enabling you to be more productive in using these frequently used commands.

TIP Customizing the Quick Access Toolbar

As you become more familiar with Microsoft Office 2007, you might find that you need quick access to additional commands, such as Print Preview or Spelling & Grammar. You can easily customize the Quick Access Toolbar by clicking the Customize Quick Access Toolbar drop-down arrow on the right end of the toolbar and adding command buttons from the list that displays. You also can customize the toolbar by changing where it displays. If you want it closer to the document window, you can move the toolbar below the Ribbon.

A ***title bar*** displays the program name and filename at the top of a window.

The third item at the top of the screen is the ***title bar***, which displays the name of the open program and the filename at the top of a window. For example, in Figure 1.1, *chap1_case_design_solution* is the name of a document, and *Microsoft Word* is the name of the program. In Figure 1.2, *Database1* is the name of the file, and *Microsoft Access* is the name of the program.

The **Ribbon** is a large strip of visual commands that enables you to perform tasks.

(The Ribbon is the command center of the Microsoft Office 2007 interface, providing access to the functionality of the programs.)

Familiarize Yourself with the Ribbon

The second section of the Office 2007 interface is the **Ribbon**, a large strip of visual commands that displays across the screen below the Office Button, Quick Access Toolbar, and the title bar. The Ribbon is the most important section of the interface: It is the command center of the Microsoft Office 2007 interface, providing access to the functionality of the programs (see Figure 1.3).

Figure 1.3 The Ribbon

The Ribbon has three main components: tabs, groups, and commands. The following list describes each component.

Tabs, which look like folder tabs, divide the Ribbon into task-oriented categories.

- **Tabs**, which look like folder tabs, divide the Ribbon into task-oriented sections. For example, the Ribbon in Word contains these tabs: Home, Insert, Page Layout, Reference, Mailings, Review, and View. When you click the Home tab, you see a set of core commands for that program. When you click the Insert tab, you see a set of commands that enable you to insert objects, such as tables, clip art, headers, page numbers, etc.

Groups organize similar commands together within each tab.

- **Groups** organize related commands together on each tab. For example, the Home tab in Word contains these groups: Clipboard, Font, Paragraph, Styles, and Editing. These groups help organize related commands together so that you can find them easily. For example, the Font group contains font-related commands, such as Font, Font Size, Bold, Italic, Underline, Highlighter, and Font Color.

A **command** is a visual icon in each group that you click to perform a task.

- **Commands** are specific tasks performed. Commands appear as visual icons or buttons within the groups on the Ribbon. The icons are designed to provide a visual clue of the purpose of the command. For example, the Bold command looks like a bolded B in the Font group on the Home tab. You simply click the desired command to perform the respective task.

The Ribbon has the same basic design—tabs, groups, and commands—across all Microsoft Office 2007 applications. When you first start using an Office 2007 application, you use the Home tab most often. The groups of commands on the Home tab are designed to get you started using the software. For example, the Home tab contains commands to help you create, edit, and format a document in Word, a worksheet in Excel, and a presentation in PowerPoint. In Access, the Home tab contains groups of commands to insert, delete, and edit records in a database table. While three of the four applications contain an Insert tab, the specific groups and commands differ by application. Regardless of the application, however, the Insert tab contains commands to *insert something*, whether it is a page number in Word, a column chart in Excel, or a shape in PowerPoint. One of the best ways to develop an understanding of the Ribbon is to study its structure in each application. As you explore each program, you will notice the similarities in how commands are grouped on tabs, and you will notice the differences specific to each application.

The Ribbon provides an extensive sets of commands that you use when creating and editing documents, worksheets, slides, tables, or other items. Figure 1.4 points out other important components of the Ribbon.

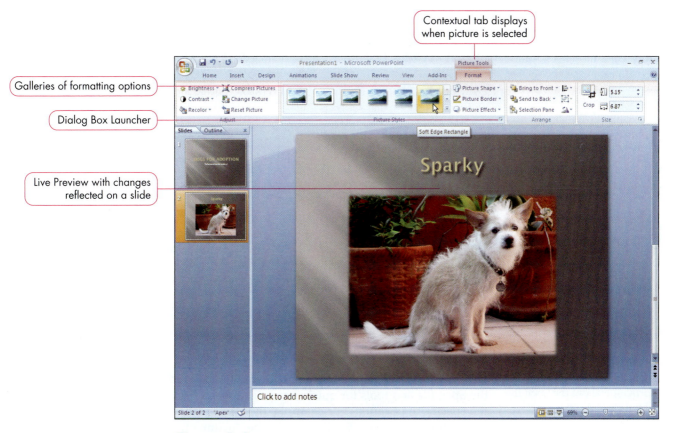

Figure 1.4 PowerPoint with Ribbon

A *dialog box* is a window that provides options related to a group of commands.

A *Dialog Box Launcher* is a small icon that, when clicked, opens a related dialog box.

A *gallery* is a set of options that appears as thumbnail graphics.

Live Preview provides a preview of the results for gallery options.

Figure 1.4 shows examples of four other components of the Ribbon. These components include a Dialog Box Launcher, a gallery, Live Preview, and a contextual tab. The following list describes each component:

- A *Dialog Box Launcher* is a small icon located on the right side of some group names that you click to open a related *dialog box*, which is a window that provides options related to a group of commands.

- A *gallery* is a set of options that appear as thumbnail graphics that visually represent the option results. For example, if you create a chart in Excel, a gallery of chart formatting options provides numerous choices for formatting the chart.

- *Live Preview* works with the galleries, providing a preview of the results of formatting in the document. As you move your mouse pointer over the gallery thumbnails, you see how each formatting option affects the selected item in your document, worksheet, or presentation. This feature increases productivity because you see the results immediately. If you do not like the results, keep moving the mouse pointer over other gallery options until you find a result you like.

A ***contextual tab*** is a tab that provides specialized commands that display only when the object they affect is selected.

- A ***contextual tab*** provides specialized commands that display only when the object they affect is selected. For example, if you insert a picture on a slide, PowerPoint displays a contextual tab on the Ribbon with commands specifically related to the selected image. When you click outside the picture to deselect it, the contextual tab disappears.

A ***Key Tip*** is the letter or number that displays over each feature on the Ribbon and Quick Access Toolbar and is the keyboard equivalent that you press.

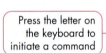

Press the letter on the keyboard to initiate a command

Figure 1.5 Key Tips Displayed for Ribbon and Quick Access Toolbar

Use the Status Bar

The ***status bar*** displays below the document and provides information about the open file and buttons for quick access.

The third major section of the Office 2007 user interface is the status bar. The ***status bar*** displays at the bottom of the program window and contains information about the open file and tools for quick access. The status bar contains details for the file in the specific application. For example, the Word status bar shows the current page, total number of pages, total words in the document, and proofreading status. The PowerPoint status bar shows the slide number, total slides in the presentation, and the applied theme. The Excel status bar provides general instructions and displays the average, count, and sum of values for selected cells. In each program, the status bar also includes View commands from the View tab for quick access. You can use the View commands to change the way the document, worksheet, or presentation displays onscreen. Table 1.2 describes the main characteristics of each Word 2007 view.

Table 1.2 Word Document Views

View Option	Characteristics
Print Layout	Displays the document as it will appear when printed.
Full Screen Reading	Displays the document on the entire screen to make reading long documents easier. To remove Full Screen Reading, press the Esc key on the keyboard.
Web Page	Displays the document as it would look as a Web page.
Outline	Displays the document as an outline.
Draft	Displays the document for quick editing without additional elements such as headers or footers.

The **Zoom slider** enables you to increase or decrease the magnification of the file onscreen.

The **Zoom slider**, located on the right edge of the status bar, enables you to drag the slide control to change the magnification of the current document, worksheet, or presentation. You can change the display to zoom in on the file to get a close up view, or you can zoom out to get an overview of the file. To use the Zoom slider, click and drag the slider control to the right to increase the zoom or to the left to decrease the zoom. If you want to set a specific zoom, such as 78%, you can type the precise value in the Zoom dialog box when you click Zoom on the View tab. Figure 1.6 shows the Zoom dialog box and the elements on Word's status bar. The Zoom dialog box in Excel and PowerPoint looks similar to the Word Zoom dialog box, but it contains fewer options in the other programs.

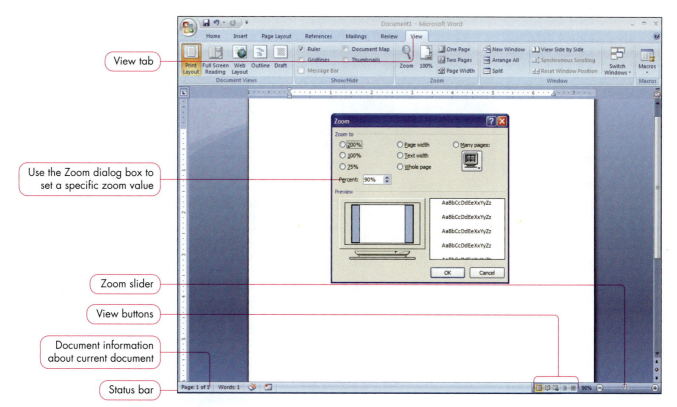

Figure 1.6 View Tab, Zoom Dialog Box, and the Status Bar in Word

Using Office 2007 Help

> Help is always available when you use any Office 2007 program.

Have you ever started a project such as assembling an entertainment center and had to abandon it because you had no way to get help when you got stuck? Microsoft Office includes features that keep this type of scenario from happening when you use Word, Excel, Access, or PowerPoint. In fact, several methods are available to locate help when you need assistance performing tasks. Help is always available when you use any Office 2007 program. Help files reside on your computer when you install Microsoft Office, and Microsoft provides additional help files on its Web site. If you link to Microsoft Office Online, you not only have access to help files for all applications, you also have access to up-to-date products, files, and graphics to help you complete projects.

Use Office 2007 Help

To access Help, press F1 on the keyboard or click the Help button on the right edge of the Ribbon shown in Figure 1.7. If you know the topic you want help with, such as printing, you can type the key term in the Search box to display help files on that topic. Help also displays general topics in the lower part of the Help window that are links to further information. To display a table of contents for the Help files, click the Show Table of Contents button, and after locating the desired help topic, you can print the information for future reference by clicking the Print button. Figure 1.7 shows these elements in Excel Help.

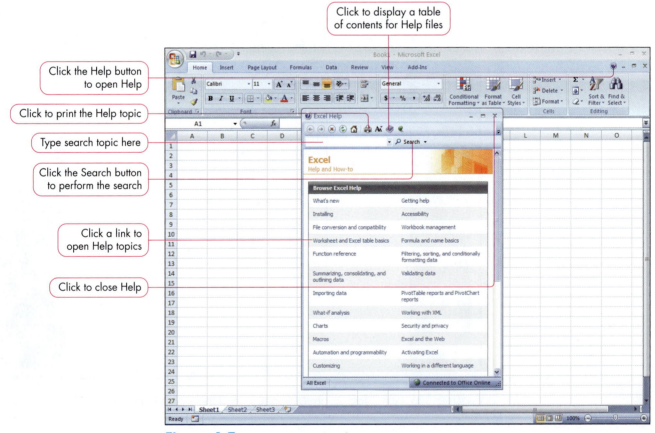

Figure 1.7 Excel Help

Use Enhanced ScreenTips

An ***Enhanced ScreenTip*** displays the name and brief description of a command when you rest the pointer on a command.

Another method for getting help is to use the Office 2007 Enhanced ScreenTips. An ***Enhanced ScreenTip*** displays when you rest the mouse pointer on a command. Notice in Figure 1.8 that the Enhanced ScreenTip provides the command name, a brief description of the command, and a link for additional help. To get help on the specific command, keep the pointer resting on the command and press F1 if the Enhanced ScreenTip displays a Help icon. The advantage of this method is that you do not have to find the correct information yourself because the Enhanced ScreenTip help is context sensitive.

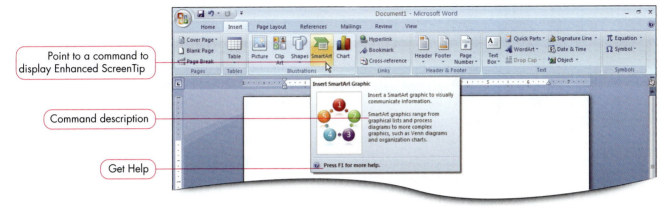

Point to a command to display Enhanced ScreenTip

Command description

Get Help

Figure 1.8 Enhanced ScreenTip

Get Help with Dialog Boxes

As you work within a dialog box, you might need help with some of the numerous options contained in that dialog box, but you do not want to close the dialog box to get assistance. For example, if you open the Insert Picture dialog box and want help with inserting files, click the Help button located on the title bar of the dialog box to display specific help for the dialog box. Figure 1.9 shows the Insert Picture dialog box with Help displayed.

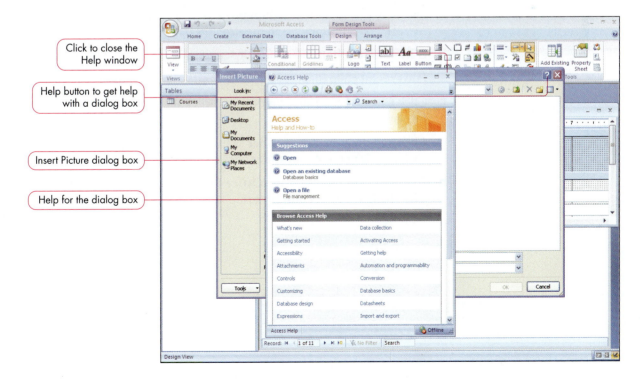

Click to close the Help window

Help button to get help with a dialog box

Insert Picture dialog box

Help for the dialog box

Figure 1.9 Help with Dialog Boxes

Hands-On Exercises

1 | Identifying Program Interface Components and Using Help

Skills covered: 1. Use PowerPoint's Office Button, Get Help in a Dialog Box, and Use the Zoom Slider **2.** Use Excel's Ribbon, Get Help from an Enhanced ScreenTip, and Use the Zoom Dialog Box **3.** Search Help in Access **4.** Use Word's Status Bar **5.** Search Help and Print a Help Topic

---

Step 1
Use PowerPoint's Office Button, Get Help in a Dialog Box, and Use the Zoom Slider

Refer to Figure 1.10 as you complete Step 1.

a. Click **Start** to display the Start menu. Click (or point to) **All Programs**, click **Microsoft Office**, then click **Microsoft Office PowerPoint 2007** to start the program.

b. Point to and rest the mouse on the Office Button and then do the same to the Quick Access Toolbar.

As you rest the mouse pointer on each object, you see an Enhanced ScreenTip for that object.

TROUBLESHOOTING: If you do not see the Enhanced ScreenTip, keep the mouse pointer on the object a little longer.

c. Click the **Office Button** and slowly move your mouse down the list of menu options, pointing to the arrow after any command name that has one.

The Office menu displays, and as you move the mouse down the list, submenus display for menu options that have an arrow.

d. Select **New**.

The New Presentation dialog box displays. Depending on how Microsoft Office 2007 was installed, your screen may vary. If Microsoft Office 2007 was fully installed, you should see a thumbnail to create a Blank Presentation, and you may see additional thumbnails in the *Recently Used Templates* section of the dialog box.

e. Click the **Help button** on the title bar of the New Presentation dialog box.

PowerPoint Help displays the topic *Create a new file from a template*.

f. Click **Close** on the Help Window and click the **Cancel** button in the New Presentation dialog box.

g. Click and drag the **Zoom slider** to the right to increase the magnification. Then click and drag the **Zoom slider** back to the center point for a 100% zoom.

h. To exit PowerPoint, click the **Office Button** to display the Office menu and then click the **Exit PowerPoint button**.

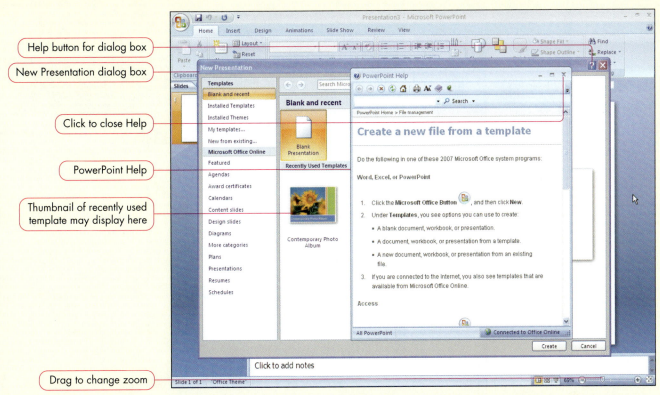

Help button for dialog box

New Presentation dialog box

Click to close Help

PowerPoint Help

Thumbnail of recently used template may display here

Drag to change zoom

Figure 1.10 PowerPoint Help for New Presentations Dialog Box

Step 2

Use Excel's Ribbon, Get Help from an Enhanced ScreenTip, and Use the Zoom Dialog Box

Refer to Figure 1.11 as you complete Step 2.

a. Click **Start** to display the Start menu. Click (or point to) **All Programs**, click **Microsoft Office**, then click **Microsoft Office Excel 2007** to open the program.

b. Click the **Insert tab** on the Ribbon.

The Insert tab contains groups of commands for inserting objects, such as tables, illustrations, charts, links, and text.

c. Rest the mouse on **Hyperlink** in the Links group on the Insert tab.

The Enhanced ScreenTip for Hyperlinks displays. Notice the Enhanced ScreenTip contains a Help icon.

d. Press **F1** on the keyboard.

Excel Help displays the *Create or remove a hyperlink* Help topic.

TROUBLESHOOTING: If you are not connected to the Internet, you might not see the context-sensitive help.

e. Click the **Close button** on the Help window.

f. Click the **View tab** on the Ribbon and click **Zoom** in the Zoom group.

The Zoom dialog box appears so that you can change the zoom percentage.

g. Click the **200%** option and click **OK**.

The worksheet is now magnified to 200% of its regular size.

h. Click **Zoom** in the Zoom group on the View tab, click the **100%** option, and click **OK**.

The worksheet is now restored to 100%.

i. To exit Excel, click the **Office Button** to display the Office menu and then click the **Exit Excel button**.

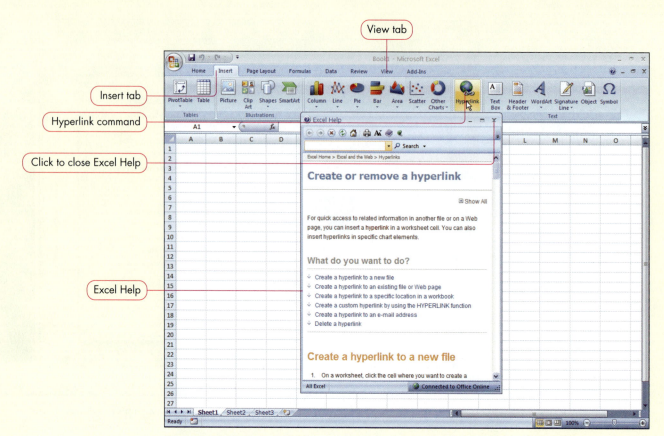

Figure 1.11 Excel Ribbon with Help

The labels on the figure:
- View tab
- Insert tab
- Hyperlink command
- Click to close Excel Help
- Excel Help

Step 3

Search Help in Access

Refer to Figure 1.12 as you complete Step 3.

a. Click **Start** to display the Start menu. Click (or point to) **All Programs**, click **Microsoft Office**, then click **Microsoft Office Access 2007** to start the program.

Access opens and displays the Getting Started with Microsoft Access screen.

TROUBLESHOOTING: If you are not familiar with Access, just use the opening screen that displays and continue with the exercise.

b. Press **F1** on the keyboard.

Access Help displays.

c. Type **table** in the Search box in the Access Help window.

d. Click the **Search** button.

Access displays help topics.

e. Click the topic **Create tables in a database**.

The help topic displays.

f. Click the **Close** button on the Access Help window.

Access Help closes.

g. To exit Access, click the **Office Button** to display the Office menu and then click the **Exit Access button**.

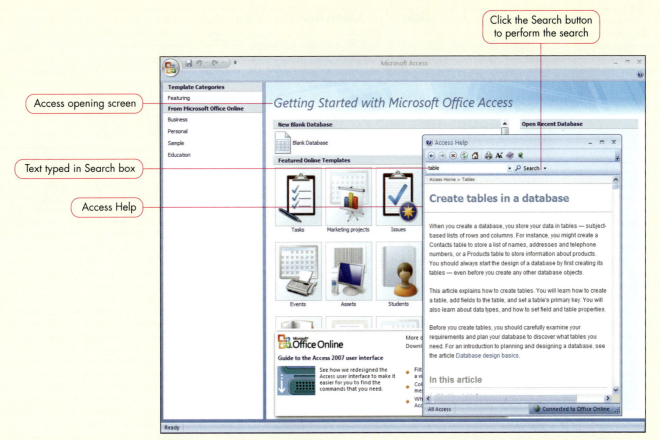

Figure 1.12 Access Help

<table>
<tr><td>

Step 4

Use Word's Status Bar

</td><td>

Refer to Figure 1.13 as you complete Step 4.

a. Click **Start** to display the Start menu. Click (or point to) **All Programs**, click **Microsoft Office**, then click **Microsoft Office Word 2007** to start the program.

Word opens with a blank document ready for you to start typing.

b. Type your first name.

Your first name displays in the document window.

c. Point your mouse to the **Zoom slider** on the status bar.

d. Click and drag the **Zoom slider** to the right to increase the magnification.

The document with your first name increases in size onscreen.

e. Click and drag the slider control to the left to decrease the magnification.

The document with your first name decreases in size.

f. Click and drag the **Zoom slider** back to the center.

The document returns to 100% magnification.

g. Slowly point the mouse to the buttons on the status bar.

A ScreenTip displays the names of the buttons.

</td></tr>
</table>

h. Click the **Full Screen Reading button** on the status bar.

The screen display changes to Full Screen Reading view.

i. Press **Esc** on the keyboard to return the display to Print Layout view.

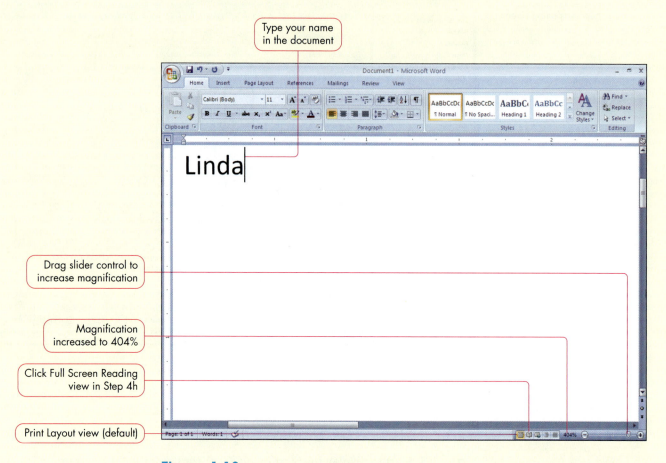

Type your name
in the document

Linda

Drag slider control to
increase magnification

Magnification
increased to 404%

Click Full Screen Reading
view in Step 4h

Print Layout view (default)

Figure 1.13 The Word Status Bar

Step 5
Search Help and Print a Help Topic

Refer to Figure 1.14 as you complete Step 5.

a. With Word open on the screen, press **F1** on the keyboard.

Word Help displays.

b. Type **zoom** in the Search box in the Word Help window.

c. Click the **Search** button.

Word Help displays related topics.

d. Click the topic **Zoom in or out of a document**.

The help topic displays.

TROUBLESHOOTING: If you do not have a printer that is ready to print, skip Step 5e and continue with the exercise.

e. Turn on the attached printer, be sure it has paper, and then click the Word Help **Print** button.

The Help topic prints on the attached printer.

f. Click the **Show Table of Contents** button on the Word Help toolbar.

The Table of Contents pane displays on the left side of the Word Help dialog box so that you can click popular Help topics, such as *What's new*. You can click a closed book icon to see specific topics to click for additional information, and you can click an open book icon to close the main Help topic.

g. Click the **Close** button on Word Help.

Word Help closes.

h. To exit Word, click the **Office Button** to display the Office menu and then click the **Exit Word button**.

A warning appears stating that you have not saved changes to your document.

i. Click **No** in the Word warning box.

You exit Word without saving the document.

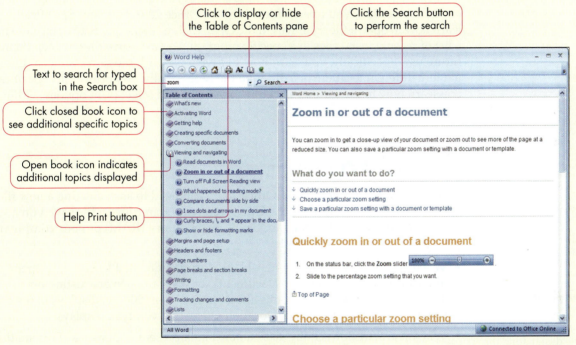

Figure 1.14 Word Help

Universal Tasks

One of the most useful and important aspects of using computers is the ability to save and re-use information. For example, you can store letters, reports, budgets, presentations, and databases as files to reopen and use at some time in the future. Today, storing large amounts of information on a computer is taken for granted, but in reality computers would not have become very important if you could not save and re-use the files you create.

Three fundamental tasks are so important for productivity that they are considered universal to most every computer program, including Office 2007:

- opening files that have been saved
- saving files you create
- printing files

In this section, you open a file within an Office 2007 program. Specifically, you learn how to open a file from within the Open dialog box and how to open a file from a list of recently used files in a specific program. You also save files to keep them for future use. Specifically, you learn how to save a file with the same name, a different name, a different location, or a different file type. Finally, you print a file. Specifically, you learn how to preview a file before printing it and select print options within the Print dialog box.

Opening a File

When you start any program in Office 2007, you need to start creating a new file or open an existing one. You use the Open command to retrieve a file saved on a storage device and place it in the random access memory (RAM) of your computer so you can work on it. For example:

The *insertion point* is the blinking vertical line in the document, cell, slide show, or database table designating the current location where text you type displays.

- When you start Word 2007, a new blank document named Document1 opens. You can either start typing in Document1, or you can open an existing document. The *insertion point*, which looks like a blinking vertical line, displays in the document designating the current location where text you type displays.
- When you start PowerPoint 2007, a new blank presentation named Presentation1 opens. You can either start creating a new slide for the blank presentation, or you can open an existing presentation.
- When you start Excel 2007, a new blank workbook named Book1 opens. You can either start inputting labels and values into Book1, or you can open an existing workbook.
- When you start Access 2007—unlike Word, PowerPoint, and Excel—a new blank database is not created automatically for you. In order to get started using Access, you must create and name a database first or open an existing database.

Open a File Using the Open Dialog Box

Opening a file in any of the Office 2007 applications is an easy process: Use the Open command from the Office menu and specify the file to open. However, locating the file to open can be difficult at times because you might not know where the file you want to use is located. You can open files stored on your computer or on a remote computer that you have access to. Further, files are saved in folders, and you might need to look for files located within folders or subfolders. The Open dialog box, shown in Figure 1.15, contains many features designed for file management; however, two features are designed specifically to help you locate files.

- **Look in**—provides a hierarchical view of the structure of folders and subfolders on your computer or on any computer network you are attached to. Move up or down in the structure to find a specific location or folder and then click the desired location to select it. The file list in the center of the dialog box displays the subfolders and files saved in the location you select. Table 1.3 lists and describes the toolbar buttons.

- **My Places bar**—provides a list of shortcut links to specific folders on your computer and locations on a computer network that you are attached to. Click a link to select it, and the file list changes to display subfolders and files in that location.

Table 1.3 Toolbar Buttons

Buttons	Characteristics
Previous Folder	Returns to the previous folder you viewed.
Up One Level	Moves up one level in the folder structure from the current folder.
Delete	Deletes the selected file or selected folder.
Create New Folder	Creates a new folder within the current folder.
Views	Changes the way the list of folders and files displays in the File list.

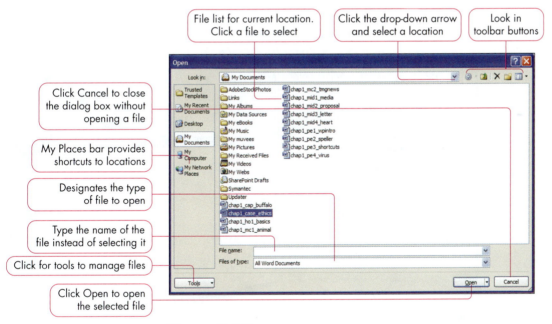

Figure 1.15 Open Dialog Box in Word

After you locate and select the file, click the Open button in the dialog box to display the file on the screen. However, if, for example, you work as part of a workgroup that shares files with each other, you might find the need to open files in a more specialized way. Microsoft Office programs provide several options for opening files when you click the drop-down arrow on the Open button. For example, if you want to keep the original file intact, you might open the file as a copy of the original. Table 1.4 describes the Open options.

Table 1.4 Open Options

Open Options	Characteristics
Open	Opens the selected file with the ability to read and write (edit).
Open Read-Only	Opens the selected file with the ability to read the contents but prevents you from changing or editing it.
Open as Copy	Opens the selected file as a copy of the original so that if you edit the file, the original remains unchanged.
Open in Browser	Opens the selected file in a Web browser.
Open with Transform	Opens a file and provides the ability to transform it into another type of document, such as an HTML document.
Open and Repair	Opens the selected file and attempts to repair any damage. If you have difficulty opening a file, try to open it by selecting Open and Repair.

Open Files Using the Recent Documents List

Office 2007 provides a quick method for accessing files you used recently. The Recent Documents list displays when the Office menu opens and provides a list of links to the last few files you used. The list changes as you work in the application to reflect only the most recent files. Figure 1.16 shows the Office menu with the Recent Documents list.

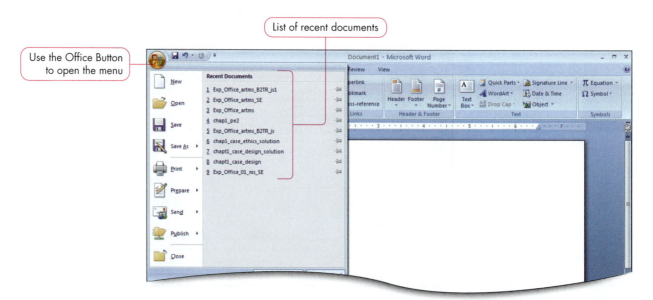

Figure 1.16 The Recent Documents List

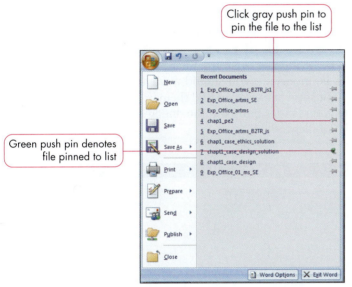

Click gray push pin to pin the file to the list

Green push pin denotes file pinned to list

Figure 1.17   The Recent Documents List

Saving a File

As you work with any Office 2007 application and create files, you will need to save them for future use. While you are working on a file, it is stored in the temporary memory or RAM of your computer. When you save a file, the contents of the file stored in RAM are saved to the hard drive of your computer or to a storage device such as a flash drive. As you create, edit, and format a complex file such as a report, slide show, or budget, you should consider saving several versions of it as you work. For example, you might number versions or use the date in the filename to designate each version. Using this method enables you to revert to a previous version of the document if necessary. To save a file you create in Word, PowerPoint, or Excel, click the Office Button to display the Office menu. Office provides two commands that work similarly: Save and Save As. Table 1.5 describes the characteristics of these two commands.

> As you create, edit, and format a complex file such as a report, slide show, or budget, you should consider saving several versions of it as you work.

Table 1.5 Save Options

Command	Characteristics
Save	Saves the open document: • If this is the first time the document is being saved, Office 2007 opens the Save As dialog box so that you can name the file. • If this document was saved previously, the document is automatically saved using the original filename.
Save As	Opens the Save As dialog box: • If this is the first time the document is being saved, use the Save As dialog box to name the file. • If this document was saved previously, use this option to save the file with a new name, in a new location, or as a new file type preserving the original file with its original name.

When you select the Save As command, the Save As dialog box appears (see Figure 1.18). Notice that saving and opening files are related, that the Save As dialog box looks very similar to the Open dialog box that you saw in Figure 1.15. The dialog box requires you to specify the drive or folder in which to store the file, the name of the file, and the type of file you wish the file to be saved as. Additionally, because finding saved files is important, you should always group related files together in folders, so that you or someone else can find them in a location that makes sense. You can use the Create New Folder button in the dialog box to create and name a folder, and then save related files to it.

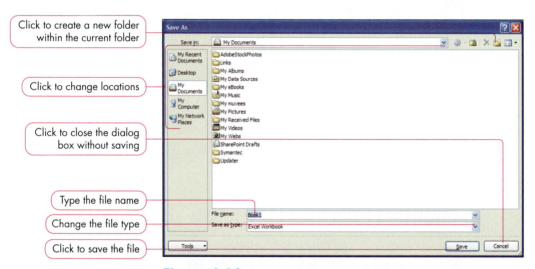

Figure 1.18 Save As Dialog Box in Excel

All subsequent executions of the Save command save the file under the assigned name, replacing the previously saved version with the new version. Pressing Ctrl+S is another way to activate the Save command. If you want to change the name of the file, use the Save As command. Word, PowerPoint, and Excel use the same basic process for saving files, which include the following options:

• naming and saving a previously unsaved file

• saving an updated file with the same name and replacing the original file with the updated one

• saving an updated file with a different name or in a different location to keep the original intact

• saving the file in a different file format

TIP   Saving from the Office Menu

You should select the Save As command on the Office menu rather than pointing to the arrow that follows the command. When you point to the arrow, menu options display for saving the file in an alternative format. Always check the Save as type box in the dialog box to be sure that the correct file type is specified.

Office 2007 saves files in a different format from previous versions of the software. Office now makes use of XML formats for files created in Word, PowerPoint, and Excel. For example, in previous versions of Word, all documents were saved with the three-letter extension .doc. Now Word saves default documents with the four-letter extension .docx. The new XML format makes use of file compression to save storage space for the user. The files are compressed automatically when saved and uncompressed when opened. Another important feature is that the XML format makes using the files you create in Office 2007 easier to open in other software. This increased portability of files is a major benefit in any workplace that might have numerous applications to deal with. The new file format also differentiates between files that contain *macros*, which are small programs that automate tasks in a file, and those that do not. This specification of files that contain macros enables a virus checker to rigorously check for damaging programs hidden in files. A *virus checker* is software that scans files for a hidden program that can damage your computer. Table 1.6 lists the file formats with the four-letter extension for Word, PowerPoint, and Excel, and a five-letter extension for Access.

A *macro* is a small program that automates tasks in a file.

A *virus checker* is software that scans files for a hidden program that can damage your computer.

A *template* is a file that contains formatting and design elements.

Table 1.6   Word, PowerPoint, Excel, and Access File Extensions

File Format	Characteristics
Word	.docx—default document format .docm—a document that contains macros .dotx—a template without macros (a **template** is a file that contains formatting and design elements) .dotm—a template with macros
PowerPoint	.pptx—default presentation format .pptm—a presentation that contains macros .potx—a template .potm—a template with macros .ppam—an add-in that contains macros .ppsx—a slide show .ppsm—a slide show with macros .sldx—a slide saved independently of a presentation .sldm—a slide saved independently of a presentation that contains a macro .thmx—a theme used to format a slide
Excel	.xlsx—default workbook .xlsm—a workbook with macros .xltx—a template .xltm—a template with a macro .xlsb—non-XML binary workbook—for previous versions of the software .xlam—an add-in that contains macros
Access	.accdb—default database

Access 2007 saves data differently from Word, PowerPoint, and Excel. When you start Access, which is a relational database, you must create a database and define at least one table for your data. Then as you work, your data is stored automatically. This powerful software enables multiple users access to up-to-date data. The concepts of saving, opening, and printing remain the same, but the process of how data is saved is unique to this powerful environment.

TIP   Changing the Display of the My Places Bar

Sometimes finding saved files can be a time-consuming chore. To help you quickly locate files, Office 2007 provides options for changing the display of the My Places bar. In Word, PowerPoint, Excel, and Access, you can create shortcuts to folders where you store commonly used files and add them to the My Places bar. From the Open or Save As dialog box, select the location in the Look in list you want to add to the bar. With the desired location selected, point to an empty space below the existing shortcuts on the My Places bar. Right-click the mouse to display a **shortcut menu**, which displays when you right-click the mouse on an object and provides a list of commands pertaining to the object you clicked. From the shortcut menu, choose Add (folder name)—the folder name is the name of the location you selected in the Look in box. The new shortcut is added to the bottom of the My Places bar. Notice the shortcut menu in Figure 1.19, which also provides options to change the order of added shortcuts or remove an unwanted shortcut. However, you can only remove the shortcuts that you add to the bar; the default shortcuts cannot be removed.

A **shortcut menu** displays when you right-click the mouse on an object and provides a list of commands pertaining to the object you clicked.

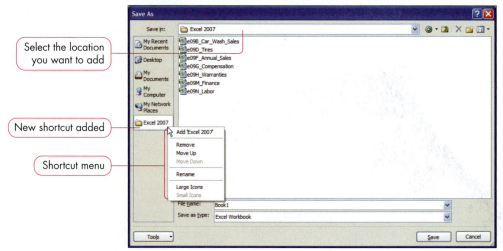

Select the location you want to add

New shortcut added

Shortcut menu

Figure 1.19 Save As Dialog Box with New Shortcut Added to My Places Bar

Printing a Document

As you work with Office 2007 applications, you will need to print hard copies of documents, such as letters to mail, presentation notes to distribute to accompany a slide show, budget spreadsheets to distribute at a staff meeting, or database summary reports to submit. Office provides flexibility so that you can preview the document before you send it to the printer; you also can select from numerous print options, such as changing the number of copies printed; or you can simply and quickly print the current document on the default printer.

Preview Before You Print

It is highly recommended that you preview your document before you print because Print Preview displays all the document elements such as graphics and formatting as they will appear when printed on paper. Previewing the document first enables you to make any changes that you need to make without wasting paper. Previewing documents uses the same method in all Office 2007 applications, that is, point to the arrow next to the Print command on the Office menu and select Print Preview to display the current document, worksheet, presentation, or database table in the Print Preview window. Figure 1.20 shows the Print Preview window in Word 2007.

> It is highly recommended that you preview your document before you print because Print Preview displays all the document elements, such as graphics and formatting, as they will appear when printed on paper.

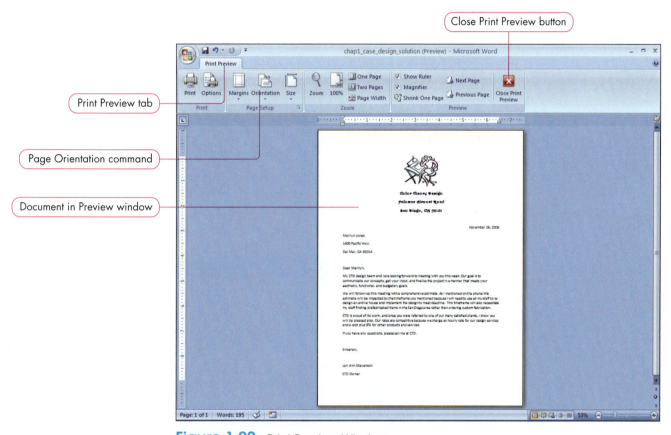

Close Print Preview button

Print Preview tab

Page Orientation command

Document in Preview window

Figure 1.20 Print Preview Window

As you preview the document, you can get a closer look at the results by changing the zoom. Notice that the mouse pointer displays in the Preview window as a magnifying glass with a plus sign, so that you can simply click in the document to increase the zoom. Once clicked, the plus sign changes to a minus sign, enabling you to click in the document again to decrease the zoom. You also can use the Zoom group on the Print Preview tab or the Zoom slider on the status bar to change the view of the document.

Other options on the Print Preview tab change depending on the application that you are using. For example, you might want to change the orientation to switch from portrait to landscape. Refer to Figure 1.20. *Portrait orientation* is longer than it is wide, like the portrait of a person; whereas, *landscape orientation* is wider than it is long, resembling a landscape scene. You also can change the size of the paper or other options from the Print Preview tab.

Portrait orientation is longer than it is wide—like the portrait of a person.

Landscape orientation is wider than it is long, resembling a landscape scene.

If you need to edit the document before printing, close the Print Preview window and return to the document. However, if you are satisfied with the document and want to print, click Print in the Print group on the Print Preview tab. The Print dialog box displays. Figure 1.21 shows Word's Print dialog box.

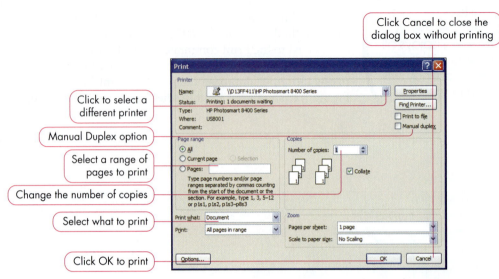

Figure 1.21 Print Dialog Box

The Print dialog box provides numerous options for selecting the correct printer, selecting what to print, and selecting how to print. Table 1.7 describes several important and often-used features of the Print dialog box.

Table 1.7 Print Dialog Box

Print Option	Characteristics
All	Select to print all the pages in the file.
Current page/slide	Select to print only the page or slide with the insertion point. This is a handy feature when you notice an error in a file, and you only want to reprint the corrected page.
Pages	Select to print only specific pages in a document. You must specify page numbers in the text box.
Number of Copies	Change the number of copies printed from the default 1 to the number desired.
Collate	Click if you are printing multiple copies of a multi-page file, and you want to print an entire first copy before printing an entire second copy, and so forth.
Print what	Select from options on what to print, varying with each application.
Selection	Select to print only selected text or objects in an Excel worksheet.
Active sheet(s)	Select to print only the active worksheet(s) in Excel.
Entire workbook	Select to print all worksheets in the Excel workbook.

As you work with other Office 2007 applications, you will notice that the main print options remain unchanged; however, the details vary based on the specific task of the application. For example, the *Print what* option in PowerPoint includes options such as printing the slide, printing handouts, printing notes, or printing an outline of the presentation.

A *duplex printer* prints on both sides of the page.

A *manual duplex* operation allows you to print on both sides of the paper by printing first on one side and then on the other.

TIP   Printing on Both Sides of the Paper

Duplex printers print on both sides of the page. However, if you do not have a duplex printer, you can still print on two sides of the paper by performing a **manual duplex** operation, which prints on both sides of the paper by printing first on one side and then on the other. To perform a manual duplex print job in Word 2007, select the Manual duplex option in the Print dialog box. Refer to Figure 1.21. With this option selected, Word prints all pages that display on one side of the paper first, then prompts you to turn the pages over and place them back in the printer tray. The print job continues by printing all the pages that appear on the other side of the paper.

Print without Previewing the File

If you want to print a file without previewing the results, select Print from the Office menu, and the Print dialog box displays. You can still make changes in the Print dialog box, or just immediately send the print job to the printer. However, if you just want to print quickly, Office 2007 provides a quick print option that enables you to send the current file to the default printer without opening the Print dialog box. This is a handy feature to use if you have only one printer attached and you want to print the current file without changing any print options. You have two ways to quick print:

- Select Quick Print from the Office menu.
- Customize the Quick Access toolbar to add the Print icon. Click the icon to print the current file without opening the Print dialog box.

Hands-On Exercises

2 | Performing Universal Tasks

Skills covered: 1. Open a File and Save It with a Different Name **2.** Use Print Preview and Select Options **3.** Print a Document

---

Step 1
Open a File and Save it with a Different Name

Refer to Figure 1.22 as you complete Step 1.

a. Start Word, click the **Office Button** to display the Office menu, and then select **Open**.

The Open dialog box displays.

b. If necessary, click the **Look in drop-down arrow** to locate the files for this textbook to find *chap1_ho2_sample*.

TROUBLESHOOTING: If you have trouble finding the files that accompany this text, you may want to ask your instructor where they are located.

c. Select the file and click **Open**.

The document displays on the screen.

d. Click the **Office Button** and then select **Save As** on the Office menu.

The Save As dialog box displays.

e. In the *File name* box, type **chap1_ho2_solution**.

f. Check the location listed in the **Save in** box. If you need to change locations to save your files, use the **Save in drop-down arrow** to select the correct location.

g. Make sure that the *Save as type* option is Word Document.

TROUBLESHOOTING: Be sure that you click the **Save As** command rather than pointing to the arrow after the command, and be sure that Word Document is specified in the Save as type box.

h. Click the **Save button** in the dialog box to save the file under the new name.

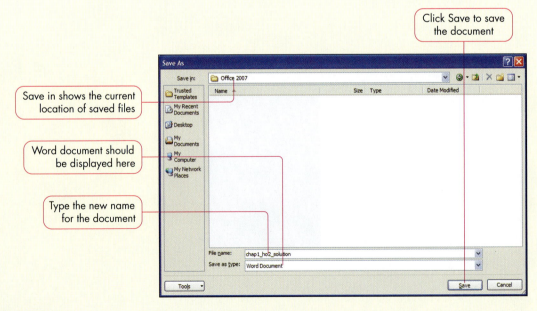

Figure 1.22 Save As Dialog Box

Step 2

Use Print Preview and Select Options

Refer to Figure 1.23 as you complete Step 2.

a. With the document displayed on the screen, click the **Office Button** and point to the arrow following **Print** on the Office menu.

The Print submenu displays.

b. Select **Print Preview**.

The document displays in the Print Preview window.

c. Point the magnifying glass mouse pointer in the document and click the mouse once.

TROUBLESHOOTING: If you do not see the magnifying glass pointer, point the mouse in the document and keep it still for a moment.

The document magnification increases.

d. Point the magnifying glass mouse pointer in the document and click the mouse again.

The document magnification decreases.

e. Click **Orientation** in the Page Setup group on the Print Preview tab.

The orientation options display.

f. Click **Landscape**.

The document orientation changes to landscape.

g. Click **Orientation** a second time and then choose **Portrait**.

The document returns to portrait orientation.

h. Click the **Close Print Preview** button on the Print Preview tab.

i. The Print Preview window closes.

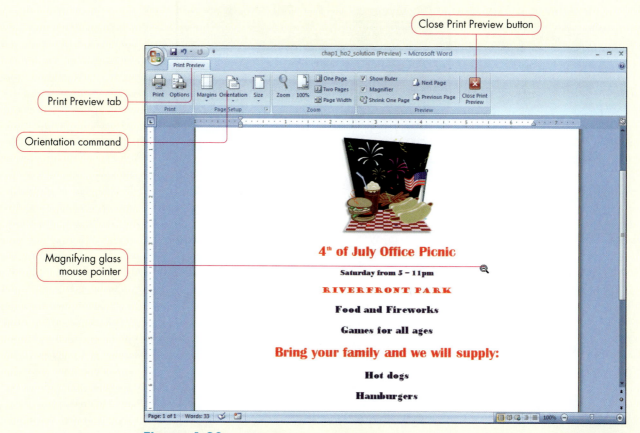

Figure 1.23 Print Preview

Refer to Figure 1.24 as you complete Step 3.

a. Click the **Office Button** and then point to the arrow next to **Print** on the Office menu.

The print options display.

b. Select **Print**.

The Print dialog box displays.

TROUBLESHOOTING: Be sure that your printer is turned on and has paper loaded.

c. If necessary, select the correct printer in the **Name box** by clicking the drop-down arrow and selecting from the resulting list.

d. Click **OK**.

The Word document prints on the selected printer.

e. To exit Word, click the **Office Button** and then click the **Exit Word button**.

f. If prompted to save the file, choose **No**.

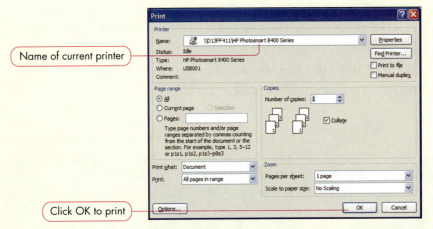

Figure 1.24 The Print Dialog Box

Basic Tasks

Many of the operations you perform in one Office program are the same or similar in all Office applications. These tasks are referred to as basic tasks and include such operations as inserting and typing over, copying and moving items, finding and replacing text, undoing and redoing commands, checking spelling and grammar, using the thesaurus, and using formatting tools. Once you learn the underlying concepts of these operations, you can apply them in different applications.

Most basic tasks in Word fall into two categories:

- editing a document
- formatting a document

Most successful writers use many word processing features to revise and edit documents, and most would agree that the revision process takes more time than the initial writing process. Errors such as spelling and grammar need to be eliminated to produce error-free writing. However, to turn a rough draft into a finished document, such as a report for a class or for a business, requires writers to revise and edit several times by adding text, removing text, replacing text, and moving text around to make the meaning clearer. Writers also improve their writing using tools to conduct research to make the information accurate and to find the most appropriate word using the thesaurus. Modern word processing applications such as Word 2007 provide these tools and more to aid the writer.

> Most successful writers use many word processing features to revise and edit documents, and most would agree that the revision process takes more time than the initial writing process.

The second category of basic tasks is formatting text in a document. Formatting text includes changing the type, the size, and appearance of text. You might want to apply formatting to simply improve the look of a document, or you might want to emphasize particular aspects of your message. Remember that a poorly formatted document or workbook probably will not be read. So whether you are creating your résumé or the income statement for a corporation's annual report, how the output looks is important. Office 2007 provides many tools for formatting documents, but in this section, you will start by learning to apply font attributes and copy those to other locations in the document.

In this section you learn to perform basic tasks in Office 2007, using Word 2007 as the model. As you progress in learning other Office programs such as PowerPoint, Excel, and Access, you will apply the same principles in other applications.

Selecting Text to Edit

Most editing processes involve identifying the text that the writer wants to work with. For example, to specify which text to edit, you must select it. The most common method used to select text is to use the mouse. Point to one end of the text you want to select (either the beginning or end) and click-and-drag over the text. The selected text displays highlighted with a light blue background so that it stands out from other text and is ready for you to work with. The *Mini toolbar* displays when you select text in Word, Excel, and PowerPoint. It displays above the selected text as semitransparent and remains semitransparent until you point to it. Often-used commands from the Clipboard, Font, and Paragraph groups on the Home tab are repeated on the Mini toolbar for quick access. Figure 1.25 shows selected text with the Mini toolbar fully displayed in the document.

The *Mini toolbar* displays above the selected text as semitransparent and repeats often-used commands.

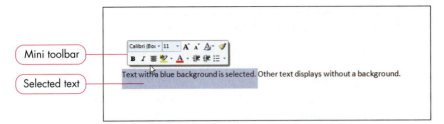

Mini toolbar

Selected text

Figure 1.25 Selected Text

Sometimes you want to select only one word or character, and trying to drag over it to select it can be frustrating. Table 1.8 describes other methods used to select text.

Table 1.8 Easy Text Selection in Word

Outcome Desired	Method
Select a word	Double-click the word.
One line of text	Point the mouse to the left of the line, and when the mouse pointer changes to a right-pointing arrow, click the mouse.
A sentence	Hold down Ctrl and click in the sentence to select.
A paragraph	Triple-click the mouse in the paragraph.
One character to the left of the insertion point	Hold down Shift and press the left arrow key.
One character to the right of the insertion point	Hold down Shift and press the right arrow key.

TIP Selecting Large Amounts of Text

As you edit documents, you might need to select a large portion of a document. However, as you click-and-drag over the text, you might have trouble stopping the selection at the desired location because the document scrolls by too quickly. This is actually a handy feature in Word 2007 that scrolls through the document when you drag the mouse pointer at the edge of the document window.

To select a large portion of a document, click the insertion point at the beginning of the desired selection. Then move the display to the end of the selection using the scroll bar at the right edge of the window. Scrolling leaves the insertion point where you placed it. When you reach the end of the text you want to select, hold down Shift and click the mouse. The entire body of text is selected.

Inserting Text and Changing to the Overtype Mode

Insert is adding text in a document.

As you create and edit documents using Word, you will need to *insert* text, which is adding text in a document. To insert or add text, point and click the mouse in the location where the text should display. With the insertion point in the location to insert the text, simply start typing. Any existing text moves to the right, making room for the new inserted text. At times you might need to add a large amount of text in a document, and you might want to replace or type over existing text instead of inserting text. This task can be accomplished two ways:

Overtype mode replaces the existing text with text you type character by character.

- Select the text to replace and start typing. The new text replaces the selected text.
- Switch to *Overtype mode*, which replaces the existing text with text you type character by character. To change to Overtype mode, select the Word Options button on the Office menu. Select the option Use Overtype Mode in the Editing Options section of the Advanced tab. Later if you want to return to Insert mode, repeat these steps to deselect the overtype mode option. Figure 1.26 shows the Word Options dialog box.

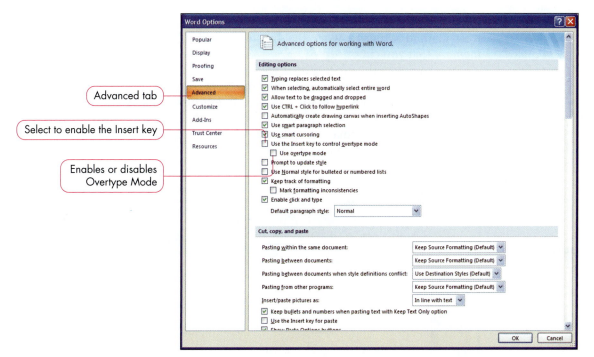

Figure 1.26 The Word Options Dialog Box

TIP Using the Insert Key on the Keyboard

If you find that you need to switch between Insert and Overtype mode often, you can enable Insert on the keyboard by clicking the Word Options button on the Office menu. Select the option Use the Insert Key to Control Overtype Mode in the Editing Options section on the Advanced tab. Refer to Figure 1.26. You can now use Insert on the keyboard to switch between the two modes, and this option stays in effect until you go back to the Word Options dialog box and deselect it.

Moving and Copying Text

As you revise a document, you might find that you need to move text from one location to another to improve the readability of the content. To move text, you must cut the selected text from its original location and then place it in the new location by pasting it there. To duplicate text, you must copy the selected text in its original location and then paste the duplicate in the desired location. To decide whether you should use the Cut or Copy command in the Clipboard group on the Home tab to perform the task, you must notice the difference in the results of each command:

- *Cut* removes the selected original text or object from its current location.
- *Copy* makes a duplicate copy of the text or object, leaving the original text or object intact.

Keep in mind while you work, that by default Office 2007 retains only the last item in memory that you cut or copied.

You complete the process by invoking the Paste command. *Paste* places the cut or copied text or object in the new location. Notice the Paste Options button displays along with the pasted text. You can simply ignore the Paste Options button, and it will disappear from the display, or you can click the drop-down arrow on the button and select a formatting option to change the display of the text you pasted. Figure 1.27 shows the options available.

Cut removes the original text or object from its current location.

Copy makes a duplicate copy of the text or object, leaving the original intact.

Paste places the cut or copied text or object in the new location.

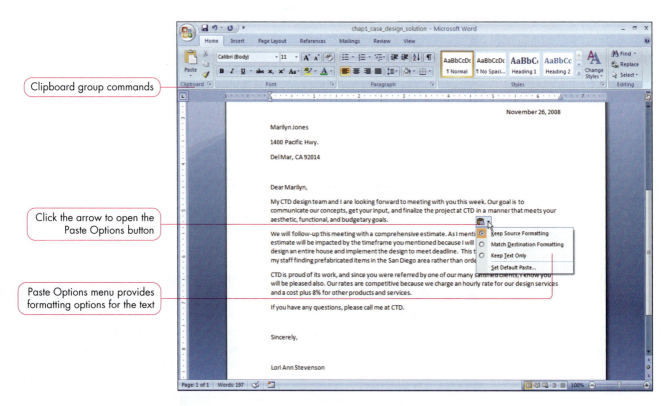

Figure 1.27 Text Pasted in the Document

Use the Office Clipboard

The **Clipboard** is a memory location that holds up to 24 items for you to paste into the current document, another file, or another application.

Office 2007 provides an option that enables you to cut or copy multiple items to the *Clipboard*, which is a memory location that holds up to 24 items for you to paste into the current file, another file, or another application. The Clipboard stays active only while you are using one of the Office 2007 applications. When you exit from all Office 2007 applications, all items on the Clipboard are deleted. To accumulate items on the Clipboard, you must first display it by clicking the Dialog Box Launcher in the Clipboard group on the Home tab. When the Clipboard pane is open on the screen, its memory location is active, and the Clipboard accumulates all items you cut or copy up to the maximum 24. To paste an item from the Clipboard, point to it, click the resulting drop-down arrow, and choose Paste. To change how the Clipboard functions, use the Options button shown in Figure 1.28. One of the most important options allows the Clipboard to accumulate items even when it is not open on the screen. To activate the Clipboard so that it works in the background, click the Options button in the Clipboard and then select Collect without Showing Office Clipboard.

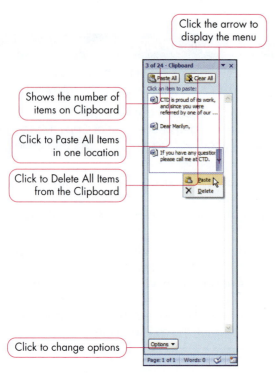

Click the arrow to display the menu

Shows the number of items on Clipboard

Click to Paste All Items in one location

Click to Delete All Items from the Clipboard

Click to change options

Figure 1.28 Clipboard

Finding, Replacing, and Going to Text

You can waste a great deal of time slowly scrolling through a document trying to locate text or other items. Office 2007 provides features that speed up editing by automatically finding text and objects in a document, thus making you more productive. Office 2007 provides the following three related operations that all use the Find and Replace dialog box:

Find locates a word or group of words in a document.

Replace not only finds text, it replaces a word or group of words with other text.

Go To moves the insertion point to a specific location in the document.

- The *Find* command enables you to locate a word or group of words in a document quickly.

- The *Replace* command not only finds text quickly, it replaces a word or group of words with other text.

- The *Go To* command moves the insertion point to a specific location in the document.

Find Text

To locate text in an Office file, choose the Find command in the Editing group on the Home tab and type the text you want to locate in the resulting dialog box, as shown in Figure 1.29. After you type the text to locate, you can find the next instance after the insertion point and work through the file until you find the instance of the text you were looking for. Alternatively, you can find all instances of the text in the file at one time. If you decide to find every instance at once, the Office application temporarily highlights each one, and the text stays highlighted until you perform another operation in the file.

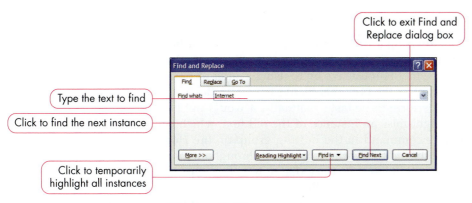

Click to exit Find and Replace dialog box

Type the text to find

Click to find the next instance

Click to temporarily highlight all instances

Figure 1.29 Find Tab of the Find and Replace Dialog Box

TIP Finding and Highlighting Text in Word

Sometimes temporarily highlighting all instances of text is not sufficient to help you edit the text you find. If you want Word to find all instances of specific text in a document and keep the highlighting from disappearing until you want it to, you can use the Reading Highlight option in the Find dialog box. One nice feature of this option is that even though the text remains highlighted on the screen, the document prints normally without highlighting. Figure 1.30 shows the Find and Replace dialog box with the Reading Highlight options that you use to highlight or remove the highlight from a document.

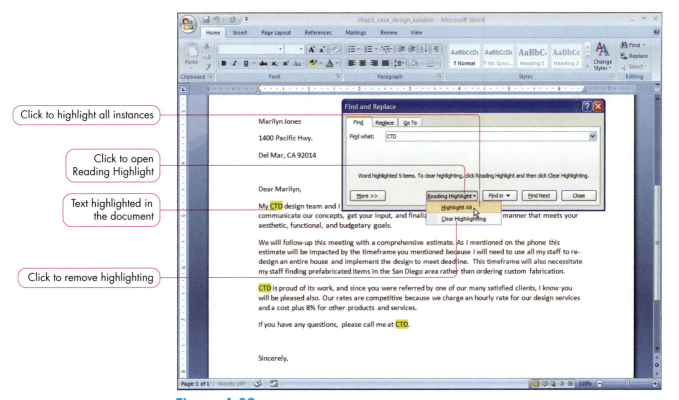

Click to highlight all instances

Click to open Reading Highlight

Text highlighted in the document

Click to remove highlighting

Figure 1.30 Find and Replace Dialog Box with Highlighting Options

Replace Text

While revising a file, you might realize that you have used an incorrect term and need to replace it throughout the entire file. Alternatively, you might realize that you could be more productive by re-using a letter or report that you polished and saved if you replace the previous client's or corporation's name with a new one. While you could perform these tasks manually, it would not be worth the time involved, and you might miss an instance of the old text, which could prove embarrassing. The Replace command in the Editing group on the Home tab can quickly and easily replace the old text with the new text throughout an entire file.

In the Find and Replace dialog box, first type the text to find, using the same process you used with the Find command. Second, type the text to replace the existing text with. Third, specify how you want Word to perform the operation. You can either replace each instance of the text individually, which can be time-consuming but allows you to decide whether to replace each instance one at a time, or you can replace every instance of the text in the document all at once. Word (but not the other Office applications) also provides options in the dialog box that help you replace only the correct text in the document. Click the More button to display these options. The most important one is the Find whole words only option. This option forces the application to find only complete words, not text that is part of other words. For instance, if you are searching for the word *off* to replace with other text, you would not want Word to replace the *off* in *office* with other text. Figure 1.31 shows these options along with the options for replacing text.

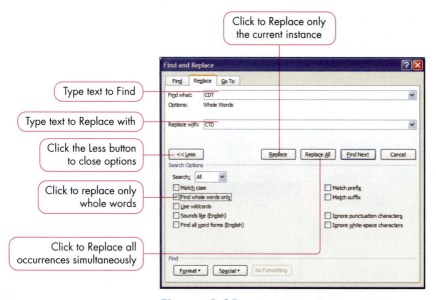

Figure 1.31 Find and Replace Dialog Box

Go Directly to a Location in a File

If you are editing a long document and want to move within it quickly, you can use the Go To command by clicking the down arrow on the Find command in the Editing group on the Home tab rather than slowly scrolling through an entire document or workbook. For example, if you want to move the insertion point to page 40 in a 200-page document, choose the Go To command and type 40 in the *Enter page number* text box. Notice the list of objects you can choose from in the Go to what section of the dialog box in Figure 1.32.

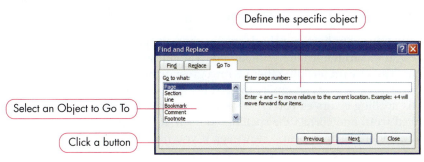

Define the specific object

Select an Object to Go To

Click a button

Figure 1.32 Go To Tab of the Find and Replace Dialog Box

Using the Undo and Redo Commands

The **Undo** command cancels your last one or more operations.

The **Redo** command reinstates or reverses an action performed by the Undo command.

As you create and edit files, you may perform an operation by mistake or simply change your mind about an edit you make. Office applications provide the **Undo** command, which can cancel your previous operation or even your last few operations. After using Undo to reverse an action or operation, you might decide that you want to use the **Redo** command to reinstate or reverse the action taken by the Undo command.

To undo the last action you performed, click Undo on the Quick Access Toolbar. For example, if you deleted text by mistake, immediately click Undo to restore it. If, however, you deleted some text and then performed several other operations, you can find the correct action to undo, with the understanding that all actions after that one will also be undone. To review a list of the last few actions you performed, click the Undo drop-down arrow and select the desired one from the list—Undo highlights all actions in the list down to that item and will undo all of the highlighted actions. Figure 1.33 shows a list of recent actions in PowerPoint. To reinstate or reverse an action as a result of using the Undo command, click Redo on the Quick Access Toolbar.

The **Repeat** command repeats only the last action you performed.

The **Repeat** command provides limited use because it repeats only the last action you performed. To repeat the last action, click Repeat on the Quick Access Toolbar. If the Office application is able to repeat your last action, the results will display in the document. Note that the Repeat command is replaced with the Redo command after you use the Undo command. For example, Figure 1.33 shows the Redo command after the Undo command has been used, and Figure 1.34 shows the Repeat command when Undo has not been used.

Click Redo to reverse an Undo command action.

Click the Undo list to find the first action to undo

Click Undo to undo the last action

Figure 1.33 Undo and Redo Buttons

Using Language Tools

Documents, spreadsheets, and presentations represent the author, so remember that errors in writing can keep people from getting a desired job, or once on the job, can keep them from getting a desired promotion. To avoid holding yourself back, you should polish your final documents before submitting them electronically or as a hard copy. Office 2007 provides built-in proofing tools to help you fix spelling and grammar errors and help you locate the correct word or information.

Check Spelling and Grammar Automatically

By default, Office applications check spelling as you type and flag potential spelling errors by underlining them with a red wavy line. Word also flags potential grammar errors by underlining them with a green wavy line. You can fix these errors as you enter text, or you can ignore the errors and fix them all at once.

To fix spelling errors as you type, simply move the insertion point to a red wavy underlined word and correct the spelling yourself. If you spell the word correctly, the red wavy underline disappears. However, if you need help figuring out the correct spelling for the flagged word, then point to the error and right-click the mouse. The shortcut menu displays with possible corrections for the error. If you find the correction on the shortcut menu, click it to replace the word in the document. To fix grammar errors, follow the same process, but when the shortcut menu displays, you can choose to view more information to see rules that apply to the potential error. Notice the errors flagged in Figure 1.34. Note that the Mini toolbar also displays automatically.

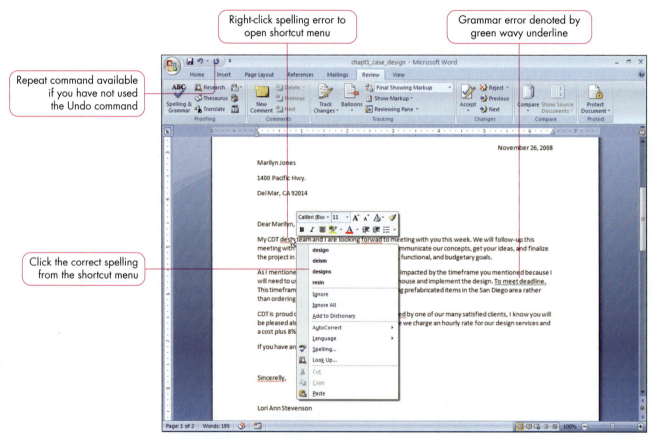

Figure 1.34 Automatic Spell and Grammar Check

Check Spelling and Grammar at Once

Some people prefer to wait until they complete typing the entire document and then check spelling and grammar at once. To check for errors, click Spelling & Grammar in Word (Spelling in Excel or PowerPoint) in the Proofing group on the Review tab. As the checking proceeds through the file and detects any spelling or grammar errors, it displays the Spelling dialog box if you are using Excel or PowerPoint, or the Spelling and Grammar dialog box in Word. You can either correct or ignore the changes that the Spelling checker proposes to your document. For example, Figure 1.35 shows the Spelling and Grammar dialog box with a misspelled word in the top section and Word's suggestions in the bottom section. Select the correction from the list and change the current instance, or you can change all instances of the error throughout the document. However, sometimes the flagged word might be a specialized term or a person's name, so if the flagged word is not a spelling error, you can ignore it once in the current document or throughout the entire document; further, you could add the word to the spell-check list so that it never flags that spelling again.

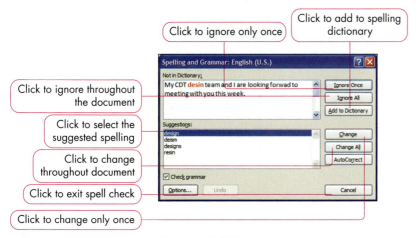

Figure 1.35 Spelling and Grammar Dialog Box

Use the Thesaurus

As you edit a document, spreadsheet, or presentation, you might want to improve your writing by finding a better or different word for a particular situation. For example, say you are stuck and cannot think of a better word for *big*, and you would like to find an alternative word that means the same. Word, Excel, and PowerPoint provide a built-in thesaurus, which is an electronic version of a book of synonyms. Synonyms are different words with the same or similar meaning, and antonyms are words with the opposite meaning.

The easiest method for accessing the Thesaurus is to point to the word in the file that you want to find an alternative for and right-click the mouse. When the shortcut menu displays, point to Synonyms, and the program displays a list of alternatives. Notice the shortcut menu and list of synonyms in Figure 1.36. To select one of the alternative words on the list, click it, and the word you select replaces the original word. If you do not see an alternative on the list that you want to use and you want to investigate further, click Thesaurus on the shortcut menu to open the full Thesaurus.

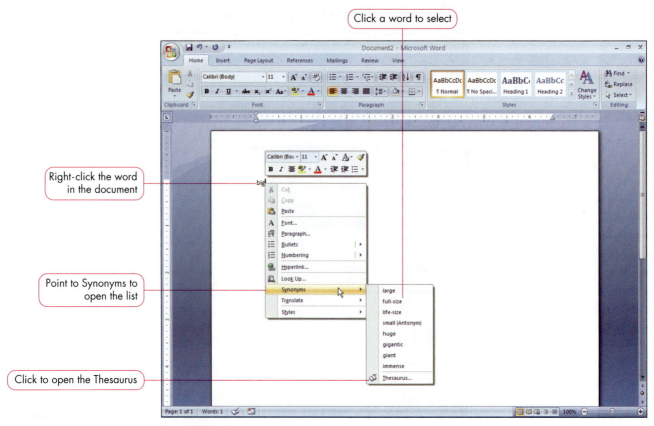

Click a word to select

Right-click the word in the document

Point to Synonyms to open the list

Click to open the Thesaurus

Figure 1.36 Shortcut Menu with Synonyms

An alternative method for opening the full Thesaurus is to place the insertion point in the word you want to look up and then click the Thesaurus command in the Proofing group on the Review tab. The Thesaurus opens with alternatives for the selected word. You can use one of the words presented in the pane, or you can look up additional words. If you do not find the word you want, use the Search option to find more alternatives. Figure 1.37 shows the Thesaurus.

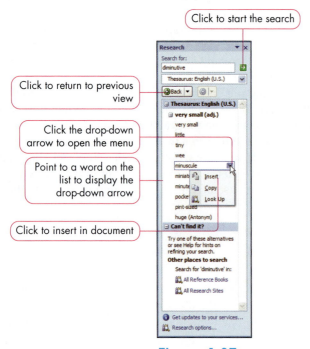

Click to start the search

Click to return to previous view

Click the drop-down arrow to open the menu

Point to a word on the list to display the drop-down arrow

Click to insert in document

Figure 1.37 The Thesaurus

Conduct Research

As you work in Word, Excel, or PowerPoint, you might need to find the definition of a word or look up an item in the encyclopedia to include accurate information. Office 2007 provides quick access to research tools. To access research tools, click the Research button in the Proofing group on the Review tab. Notice in Figure 1.38 that you can specify what you want to research and specify where to Search. Using this feature, you can choose from reference books, research sites, and business and financial sites.

Click to start searching

Type what you want to research

Click the down arrow and select where to search

Results of search

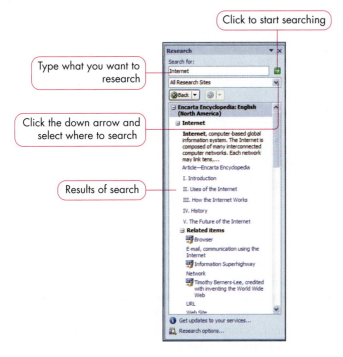

Figure 1.38 Research Task Pane

 TIP Avoiding Plagiarism

If you use the research feature in Office to find information in an encyclopedia or in other locations to help you create your document, then you need to credit the source of that information. Avoid the problem of plagiarism, which is borrowing other people's words or ideas, by citing all sources that you use. You might want to check with your instructor for the exact format for citing sources.

Applying Font Attributes

Taking the time to format text helps the reader find important information in the document by making it stand out and helps the reader understand the message by emphasizing key items.

After you have edited a document, you might want to improve its visual appeal by formatting the text. *Formatting text* changes an individual letter, a word, or a body of selected text. Taking the time to format text helps the reader find important information in the document by making it stand out and helps the reader understand the message by emphasizing key items. You can format the text in the document by changing the following font attributes:

Formatting text changes an individual letter, a word, or a body of selected text.

- Font face or size
- Font attributes such as bold, underline, or italic
- Font color

The Font group on the Home tab—available in Word, Excel, PowerPoint, and Access—provides many formatting options, and Office provides two methods for applying these font attributes:

- Choose the font attributes first and then type the text. The text displays in the document with the formatting.

- Type the text, select the text to format, and choose the font attributes. The selected text displays with the formatting.

You can apply more than one attribute to text, so you can select one or more attributes either all at once or at any time. Also it is easy to see which attributes you have applied to text in the document. Select the formatted text and look at the commands in the Font group on the Home tab. The commands in effect display with a gold background. See Figure 1.39. To remove an effect from text, select it and click the command. The gold background disappears for attributes that are no longer in effect.

Gold background denotes attributes used to format text

Figure 1.39   Font Group of the Home tab

Change the Font

A ***font*** is a named set of characters with the same design.

A ***font*** is a named set of characters with the same design, and Office 2007 provides many built-in fonts for you to choose from. Remember that more is not always better when applied to fonts, so limit the number of font changes in your document. Additionally, the choice of a font should depend on the intent of the document and should never overpower the message. For example, using a fancy or highly stylized font that may be difficult to read for a client letter might seem odd to the person receiving it and overpower the intended message.

Remember that more is not always better when applied to fonts, so limit the number of font changes in your document.

One powerful feature of Office 2007 that can help you decide how a font will look in your document is Live Preview. First select the existing text, and then click the drop-down arrow on the Font list in the Font group on the Home tab. As you point to a font name in the list, Live Preview changes the selected text in the document to that font. Figure 1.40 shows the selected text displaying in a different font as a result of Live Preview.

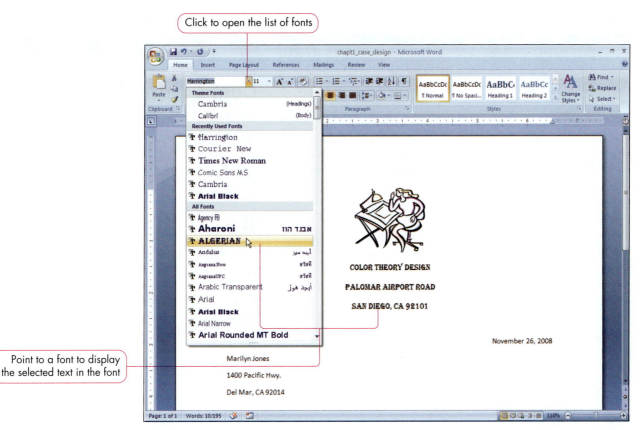

Figure 1.40 Font List

Change the Font Size, Color, and Attributes

Besides changing the font, you also can change the size, color, and other attributes of text in a document. Because these formatting operations are used so frequently, Office places many of these commands in several places for easy access:

- in the Font group on the Home tab
- on the Mini toolbar
- in the Font dialog box

Table 1.9 describes the commands that display in the Font group of the Home tab and in the Font dialog box.

Table 1.9 Font Commands

Command	Description	Example
Font	Enables you to designate the font.	Arial **Comic Sans MS**
Font Size	Enables you to designate an exact font size.	Size 8 Size 18
Grow Font	Each time you click the command, the selected text increases one size.	A **A**
Shrink Font	Each time you click the command, the selected text decreases one size.	B B
Clear Formatting	Removes all formatting from the selected text.	*Formatted* Cleared
Bold	Makes the text darker than the surrounding text.	**Bold**
Italic	Places the selected text in italic, that is, slants the letters to the right.	*Italic*
Underline	Places a line under the text. Click the drop-down arrow to change the underline style.	<u>Underline</u>
Strikethrough	Draws a line through the middle of the text.	~~Strikethrough~~
Subscript	Places selected text below the baseline.	Sub$_{script}$
Superscript	Places selected text above the line of letters.	Super^{script}
Change Case	Changes the case of the selected text. Click the drop-down arrow to select the desired case.	lowercase UPPERCASE
Text Highlight Color	Makes selected text look like it was highlighted with a marker pen. Click the drop-down arrow to change color and other options.	Highlighted
Font Color	Changes the color of selected text. Click the drop-down arrow to change colors.	Font Color

If you have several formatting changes to make, click the Dialog Box Launcher in the Font group on the Home tab to display the Font dialog box. The Font dialog box is handy because all the formatting features display in one location, and it provides additional options such as changing the underline color. Figure 1.41 shows the Font dialog box in Word.

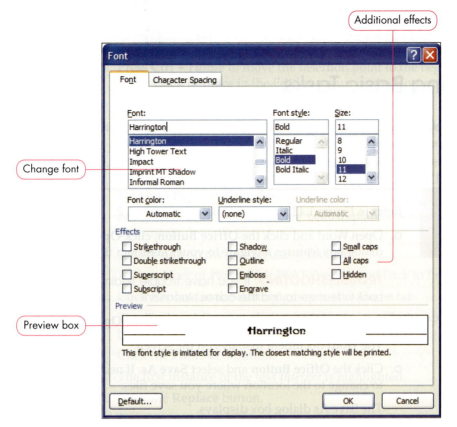

Figure 1.41 Font Dialog Box

Copying Formats with the Format Painter

After formatting text in one part of a document, you might want to apply that same formatting to other text in a different location in the document. You could try to remember all the formatting options you selected, but that process would be time-consuming and could produce inconsistent results. Office 2007 provides a shortcut method called the *Format Painter*, which copies the formatting of text from one location to another.

The *Format Painter* copies the formatting of text from one location to another.

Select the formatted text you want to copy and click the Format Painter in the Clipboard group on the Home tab to copy the format. Single-click the command to turn it on to copy formatting to one location—the option turns off automatically after one copy—or double-click the command to turn it on for unlimited format copying—you must press Esc on the keyboard to turn it off.

Multiple Choice Continued...

13. Word flags misspelled words by marking them with which one of the following?

(a) A green wavy underline
(b) Boldfacing them
(c) A red wavy underline
(d) A double-underline in black

14. Which of the following displays when you select text in a document?

(a) The Mini toolbar
(b) The Quick Access Toolbar
(c) A shortcut menu
(d) The Ribbon

15. Formatting text allows you to change which of the following text attributes?

(a) The font
(b) The font size
(c) The font type
(d) All of the above

Practice Exercises

1 Using Help and Print Preview in Access 2007

a. Open Access. Click the **Office Button** and then select **Open**. Use the Look in feature to find the *chap1_pe1* database and then click **Open**.

b. At the right side of the Ribbon, click the **Help** button. In the Help window, type **table** in the **Type words to search for** box. Click the **Search** button.

c. Click the topic *Create tables in a database*. Browse the content of the Help window and then click the **Close** button in the Help window.

d. Double-click the **Courses table** in the left pane. The table opens in Datasheet view.

e. Click the **Office Button**, point to the arrow after the **Print** command, and select **Print Preview** to open the Print Preview window with the Courses table displayed.

f. Point the mouse pointer on the table and click to magnify the display. Compare your screen to Figure 1.45.

g. Click the **Close Print Preview** button on the Print Preview tab.

h. Click the **Office Button** and then click the **Exit Access button**.

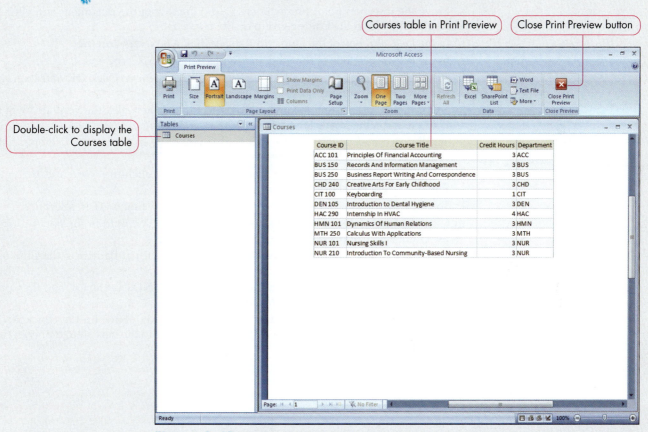

Figure 1.45 Access Print Preview

...continued on Next Page

Practice Exercises | Office Fundamentals 57

As part of your Introduction to Computers course, you have prepared an oral report on phishing. You want to provide class members with a handout that summarizes the main points of your report. This handout is in the rough stages, so you need to edit it, and you also realize that you can format some of the text to emphasize the main points.

a. Start Word. Click the **Office Button** and then select **Open**. Use the *Look in* feature to find the *chap1_pe2* document and then click **Open**.

b. Click the **Office Button** and then select **Save As**. In the *File name* box, type the document name, **chap1_pe2_solution**, be sure that Word document displays in the *Save as type* box, and use the *Look in* option to move to the location where you save your class files. Click **Save**.

c. In the document, click after the word Name and type **your name**.

d. Select your name and then click **Bold** and **Italic** on the Mini toolbar—remember to point to the Mini toolbar to make it display fully. Your name displays in bold and italic.

e. Move the insertion point immediately before the title of the document and click the **Replace** button in the Editing group on the Home tab.

f. In the *Find what* box of the Find and Replace dialog box, type **internet**.

g. In the *Replace with* box of the Find and Replace dialog box, type **email**.

h. Click the **Replace All** button to have Word replace the text. Click **OK** and then click **Close** to close the dialog boxes.

i. To format the title of the document, first select it and then click the **Font arrow** in the Font group on the Home tab to display the available fonts.

j. Scroll down and choose the **Impact** font if you have it; otherwise, use one that is available.

k. Place the insertion point in the word *Phishng*. Right-click the word and then click **Phishing** from the shortcut menu.

l. To emphasize important text in the list, double-click the first **NOT** to select it.

m. Click the **Font Color** arrow and select Red, and then click **Bold** in the Font group on the Home tab to apply bold to the text.

n. With the first instance of NOT selected, double-click **Format Painter** in the Clipboard group on the Home tab.

o. Double-click the second and then the third instance of **NOT** in the list, and then press **Esc** on the keyboard to turn off the Format Painter.

p. Compare your document to Figure 1.46. Save by clicking **Save** on the Quick Access Toolbar. Close the document and exit Word or proceed to the next step to preview and print the document.

...continued on Next Page

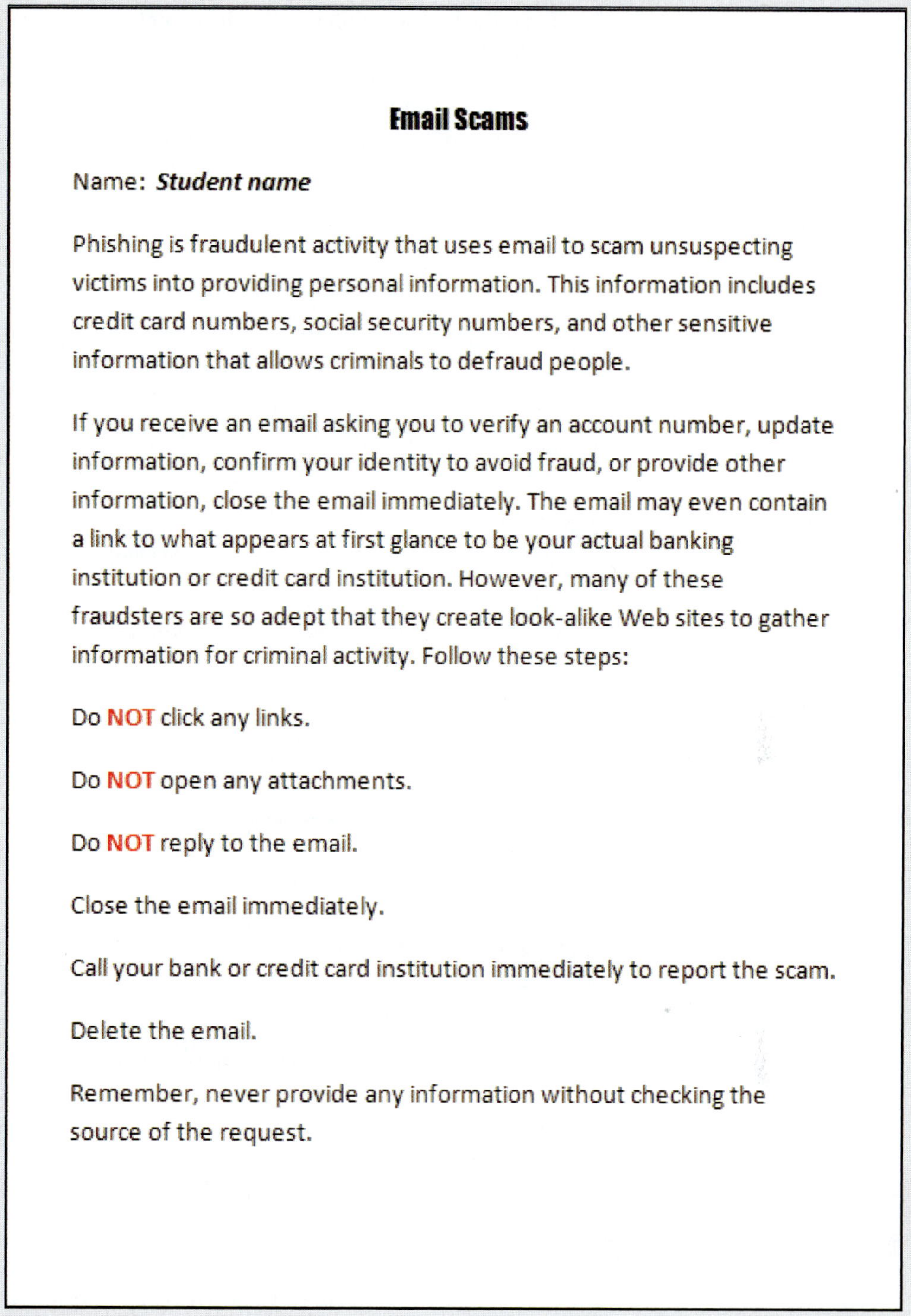

Email Scams

Name: *Student name*

Phishing is fraudulent activity that uses email to scam unsuspecting victims into providing personal information. This information includes credit card numbers, social security numbers, and other sensitive information that allows criminals to defraud people.

If you receive an email asking you to verify an account number, update information, confirm your identity to avoid fraud, or provide other information, close the email immediately. The email may even contain a link to what appears at first glance to be your actual banking institution or credit card institution. However, many of these fraudsters are so adept that they create look-alike Web sites to gather information for criminal activity. Follow these steps:

Do **NOT** click any links.

Do **NOT** open any attachments.

Do **NOT** reply to the email.

Close the email immediately.

Call your bank or credit card institution immediately to report the scam.

Delete the email.

Remember, never provide any information without checking the source of the request.

Figure 1.46 Phishing Document

3 Previewing and Printing a Document

You created a handout to accompany your oral presentation in the previous exercise. Now you want to print it out so that you can distribute it.

a. If necessary, open the *chap1_pe2_solution* that you saved in the previous exercise.
b. Click the **Office Button**, point to the arrow after the Print command, and select **Print Preview** to open the Print Preview window with the document displayed.

...continued on Next Page

c. Point the mouse pointer in the document and click to magnify the display. Click the mouse pointer a second time to reduce the display.

d. To change the orientation of the document, click **Orientation** in the Page Setup group and choose **Landscape**.

e. Click **Undo** on the Quick Access Toolbar to undo the last command, which returns the document to portrait orientation. Compare your results to the zoomed document in Figure 1.47.

f. Click **Print** on the Print Preview tab to display the Print dialog box.

g. Click **OK** to print the document.

h. Close the document without saving it.

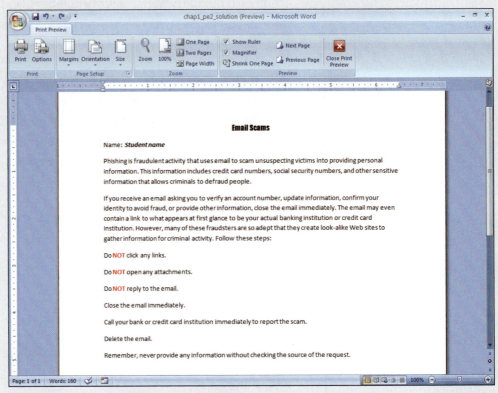

Figure 1.47 Document in Print Preview Window

4 Editing a Promotion Flyer

You work for Business Express, formerly known as Print Express, a regional company specializing in business centers that design and produce documents for local businesses and individuals. Business Express has just undergone a major transition along with a name change. Your job is to edit and refine an existing flyer to inform customers of the new changes. Proceed as follows:

a. Open Word. Click the **Office Button** and then select **Open**. Use the *Look in* feature to find the *chap1_pe4* document.

b. Click the **Office Button** again and select **Save As**. Type the document name, **chap1_pe4_solution**, be sure that Word document displays in the *Save as type* box, and use the *Look in* option to move to the location where you save your class files.

c. Place the insertion point at the beginning of the document, and then click **Spelling & Grammar** in the Proofing group on the Review tab to open the Spelling and Grammar dialog box.

d. Click the **Change** button three times to correct the spelling errors. Click **OK** to close the completion box.

...continued on Next Page

e. Place the insertion point at the end of the first sentence of the document—just before the period. To insert the following text, press **Spacebar** and type **that offers complete business solutions**.

f. Place the insertion point in *good* in the first sentence of the third paragraph and right-click the mouse.

g. Point to **Synonyms** and then click **first-rate** to replace the word in the document.

h. Place the insertion point in *bigger* in the last sentence of the third paragraph and click **Thesaurus** in the Proofing group on the Review tab. Point to **superior** and click the drop-down arrow that displays. Click **Insert** from the menu to replace the word in the document and then click the **Close** button on the Thesaurus.

i. Select the last full paragraph of the document and click **Cut** in the Clipboard group on the Home tab to remove the paragraph from the document.

j. Place the insertion point at the beginning of the new last paragraph and click **Paste** in the Clipboard group on the Home tab to display the text.

k. Click **Undo** on the Quick Access Toolbar twice to undo the paste operation and to undo the cut operation—placing the text back in its original location.

l. Place the insertion point after the colon at the bottom of the document and type **your name**.

m. Compare your results to Figure 1.48 and then save and close the document.

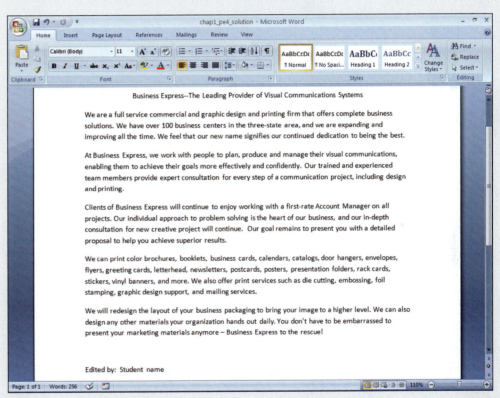

Figure 1.48 Business Flyer

Mid-Level Exercises

1 Updating a Training Document

Your position as trainer for a large building supply company involves training all new employees. It is your job to familiarize new employees with the services provided by Castle Home Building Supply. You distribute a list at the training session and you realize that it needs updating before the next session, so you decide to edit and format it.

a. Start Word. Open the *chap1_mid1* file and save it as **chap1_mid1_solution**.

b. Change the title font to Arial Rounded MT Bold size 16 and change the font color to dark brown.

c. Make the subtitle Arial Unicode MS and italic.

d. Cut the item *Help with permits* and make it the second item on the list.

e. In the first list item, insert **and** after the word *fair*.

f. Change the word *help* in the last list item to **Assistance**.

g. Select the list of items excluding the heading, Services Provided.

h. Bold the list and change the font size to 16.

i. Save the document and compare it to Figure 1.49.

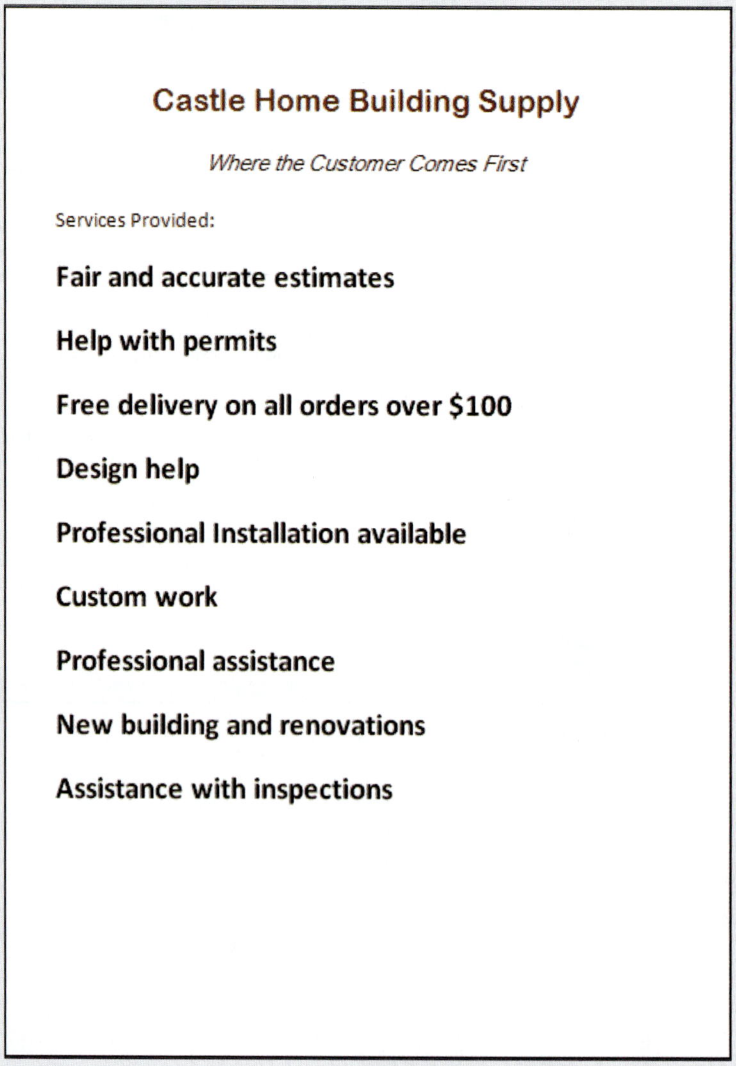

Castle Home Building Supply

Where the Customer Comes First

Services Provided:

Fair and accurate estimates

Help with permits

Free delivery on all orders over $100

Design help

Professional Installation available

Custom work

Professional assistance

New building and renovations

Assistance with inspections

Figure 1.49 Training Document

...continued on Next Page

The owner of the Bayside Restaurant wants your help formatting his menu so that it is more pleasing to customers; follow the steps below:

   a. Open the *chap1_mid2* document and save it as **chap1_mid2_solution**.

   b. Format the menu title as Broadway size 16.

   c. Format the three headings: Appetizers, Soups and Salads, and Lunch or Dinner Anytime! as Bodoni MT Black, size 12, and change the font color to Dark Red. Remember to format the first one and use the Format Painter for the second two headings.

   d. Format all the dish names, such as Nachos, using the Outline Font Effects.

   e. Bold all the prices in the document.

   f. Preview the document, compare to Figure 1.50, and then print it.

   g. Save and close the document.

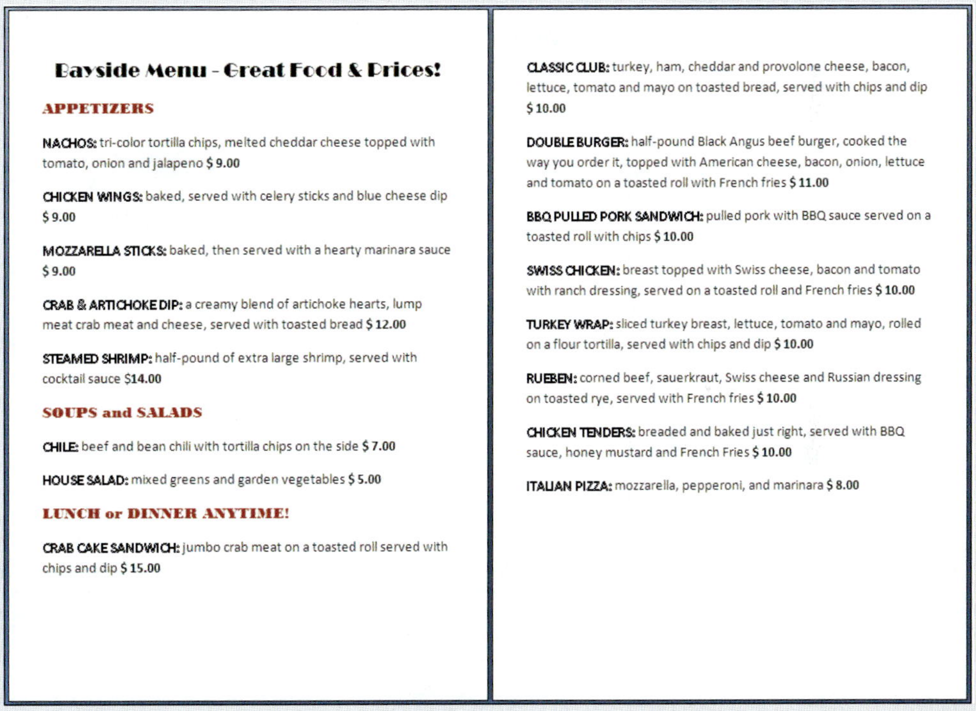

Bayside Menu - Great Food & Prices!

APPETIZERS

NACHOS: tri-color tortilla chips, melted cheddar cheese topped with tomato, onion and jalapeno **$ 9.00**

CHICKEN WINGS: baked, served with celery sticks and blue cheese dip **$ 9.00**

MOZZARELLA STICKS: baked, then served with a hearty marinara sauce **$ 9.00**

CRAB & ARTICHOKE DIP: a creamy blend of artichoke hearts, lump meat crab meat and cheese, served with toasted bread **$ 12.00**

STEAMED SHRIMP: half-pound of extra large shrimp, served with cocktail sauce **$14.00**

SOUPS and SALADS

CHILE: beef and bean chili with tortilla chips on the side **$ 7.00**

HOUSE SALAD: mixed greens and garden vegetables **$ 5.00**

LUNCH or DINNER ANYTIME!

CRAB CAKE SANDWICH: jumbo crab meat on a toasted roll served with chips and dip **$ 15.00**

CLASSIC CLUB: turkey, ham, cheddar and provolone cheese, bacon, lettuce, tomato and mayo on toasted bread, served with chips and dip **$ 10.00**

DOUBLE BURGER: half-pound Black Angus beef burger, cooked the way you order it, topped with American cheese, bacon, onion, lettuce and tomato on a toasted roll with French fries **$ 11.00**

BBQ PULLED PORK SANDWICH: pulled pork with BBQ sauce served on a toasted roll with chips **$ 10.00**

SWISS CHICKEN: breast topped with Swiss cheese, bacon and tomato with ranch dressing, served on a toasted roll and French fries **$ 10.00**

TURKEY WRAP: sliced turkey breast, lettuce, tomato and mayo, rolled on a flour tortilla, served with chips and dip **$ 10.00**

RUEBEN: corned beef, sauerkraut, Swiss cheese and Russian dressing on toasted rye, served with French fries **$ 10.00**

CHICKEN TENDERS: breaded and baked just right, served with BBQ sauce, honey mustard and French Fries **$ 10.00**

ITALIAN PIZZA: mozzarella, pepperoni, and marinara **$ 8.00**

Figure 1.50 The Formatted Menu

...continued on Next Page

Your job duties at Health First Insurance, Inc., involve maintaining the correspondence. You need to update the welcome letter you send to clients to reflect the company's new name, new address, and other important elements, and then address it to a new client. Proceed as follows.

a. Open the *chap1_mid3* document and save it as **chap1_mid3_solution**.

b. Run the Spelling check to eliminate the errors.

c. Use Replace to change **University Insurance, Inc**. to **Health First Insurance, Inc**. throughout the letter.

d. Change the Address from **123 Main St**. to **1717 N. Zapata Way**.

e. Change the inside address that now has **Client name, Client Address, Client City, State and Zip Code** to **your name and complete address**. Also change the salutation to your name.

f. Move the first paragraph so that it becomes the last paragraph in the body of the letter.

g. Preview the letter to be sure that it fits on one page, compare it with Figure 1.51, and then print it.

h. Save and close the document.

Health First Insurance, Inc.

1717 N. Zapata Way

Laredo, TX 78043

Student name

Student Address

Student City, State, and Zip Code

Dear Student name:

Welcome to the Health First Insurance, Inc. We have received and accepted your application and premium for health insurance. Please detach and the ID cards attached to this letter and keep with you at all times for identification, reference and access to emergency phone assistance and Pre Notification numbers in the event of a claim.

Enclosed you will find a Certificate of Coverage detailing the benefits, limits, exclusions and provisions of the Health First Insurance, Inc. Medical Plan. Please review the Certificate of Coverage thoroughly and contact us if you have any questions regarding the terms and provisions.

In order for you and your dependents to receive adequate medical treatment and for your assistance, the Health First Insurance, Inc. Medical Plan requires any insured (or someone on their behalf) to Pre-notify Health First Insurance, Inc., for any hospital admission prior to admittance (or within 36 hours after an emergency admission). Additionally, the Health First Insurance, Inc. Medical Plan requires all insured to utilize the provider network.

We appreciate your confidence in our organization and look forward to serving your insurance needs.

Sincerely,

Maria Fernandez

Agent

Health First Insurance, Inc.

Figure 1.51 The Updated Letter

Capstone Exercise

In this project, you work with a business plan for Far East Trading Company that will be submitted to funding sources in order to secure loans. The document requires editing to polish the final product and formatting to enhance readability and emphasize important information.

Editing the Document

This document is ready for editing, so proceed as follows:

a. Open the *chap1_cap* document. Save the document as **chap1_cap_solution**.

b. Run the Spelling and Grammar check to eliminate all spelling and grammar errors in the document.

c. Use the Thesaurus to find a synonym for the word **unique** in the second paragraph of the document.

d. Use the Go To command to move to page 3, and change the $175,000 to $250,000.

e. Move the entire second section of the document (notice the numbers preceding it) now located at the end of the document to its correct location after the first section.

f. Insert the street **1879 Columbia Ave.** before Portland in the first paragraph.

g. Copy the inserted street address to section 2.3 and place it in front of Portland there also.

h. Replace the initials **FET** with **FETC** for every instance in the document.

i. Type over 1998 in the third paragraph so that it says 2008.

Formatting the Document

Next you will apply formatting techniques to the document. These format options will further increase the readability and attractiveness of your document.

a. Select the two-line title and change the font to Engravers MT, size 14, and change the color to Dark Red.

b. Select the first heading in the document: 1.0 Executive Summary, then change the font to Gautami, bold, and change the color to Dark Blue.

c. Use the Format Painter to make all the main numbered headings the same formatting, that is 2.0, 3.0, 4.0, and 5.0.

d. The first three numbered sections have subsections such as 1.1, 1.2. Select the heading 1.1 and format it for bold, italic, and change the color to a lighter blue—Aqua, Accents, Darker 25%.

e. Use the Format Painter to make all the numbered subsections the same formatting.

Printing the Document

To finish the job, you need to print the business plan.

a. Preview the document to check your results.

b. Print the document.

c. Save your changes and close the document.

Mini Cases

Use the rubric following the case as a guide to evaluate our work, but keep in mind that your instructor may impose additional grading criteria or use a different standard to judge your work.

A Thank-You Letter

GENERAL CASE

As the new volunteer coordinator for Special Olympics in your area, you need to send out information for prospective volunteers, and the letter you were given needs editing and formatting. Open the *chap1_mc1* document and make necessary changes to improve the appearance. You should use Replace to change the text (insert your state name), use the current date and your name and address information, format to make the letter more appealing, and eliminate all errors. Your finished document should be saved as **chap1_mc1_solution**.

Performance Elements	Exceeds Expectations	Meets Expectations	Below Expectations
Corrected All Errors	Document contains no errors.	Document contains minimal errors.	Document contains several errors.
Use of Character Formatting Features such as Font, Font Size, Font Color, or Other Attributes	Used character formatting options throughout entire document.	Used character formatting options in most sections of document.	Used character formatting options on a small portion of document.
Inserted Text where Instructed	The letter is complete with all required information inserted.	The letter is mostly complete.	Letter is incomplete.

The Information Request Letter

RESEARCH CASE

Search the Internet for opportunities to teach abroad or for internships available in your major. Have fun finding a dream opportunity. Use the address information you find on the Web site that interests you, and compose a letter asking for additional information. For example, you might want to teach English in China, so search for that information. Your finished document should be saved as **chap1_mc2_solution**.

Performance Elements	Exceeds Expectations	Meets Expectations	Below Expectations
Use of Character Formatting	Three or more character formats applied to text.	One or two character formats applied to text.	Does not apply character formats to text.
Language Tools	No spelling or grammar errors.	One spelling or grammar error.	More than one spelling or grammar error.
Presentation	Information is easy to read and understand.	Information is somewhat unclear.	Letter is unclear.

Movie Memorabilia

DISASTER RECOVERY

Use the following rubrics to guide your evaluation of your work, but keep in mind that your instructor may impose additional grading criteria.

Open the *chap1_mc3* document that can be found in the Exploring folder. The advertising document is over-formatted, and it contains several errors and problems. For example, the text has been formatted in many fonts that are difficult to read. The light color of the text also has made the document difficult to read. You should improve the formatting so that it is consistent, helps the audience read the document, and is pleasing to look at. Your finished document should be saved as **chap1_mc3_solution**.

Performance Elements	Exceeds Expectations	Meets Expectations	Below Expectations
Type of Font Chosen to Format Document	Number and style of fonts appropriate for short document.	Number or style of fonts appropriate for short document.	Overused number of fonts or chose inappropriate font.
Color of Font Chosen to Format Document	Appropriate font colors for document.	Most font colors appropriate.	Overuse of font colors.
Overall Document Appeal	Document looks appealing.	Document mostly looks appealing.	Did not improve document much.

Introduction to Access

Finding Your Way through a Database

Objectives

After reading this chapter, you will be able to:

1. Explore, describe, and navigate among the objects in an Access database **(page 71)**.

2. Understand the difference between working in storage and memory **(page 78)**.

3. Practice good file management **(page 79)**.

4. Back up, compact, and repair Access files **(page 80)**.

5. Create filters **(page 89)**.

6. Sort table data on one or more fields **(page 92)**.

7. Know when to use Access or Excel to manage data **(page 94)**.

8. Use the Relationship window **(page 102)**.

9. Understand relational power **(page 103)**.

Hands-On Exercises

Exercises	Skills Covered
1. **INTRODUCTION TO DATABASES (page 81)** **Open:** chap1_ho1-3_traders.accdb **Copy, rename, and backup:** chap1_ho1-3_traders_solution.accdb chap1_ho1_traders_solution.accdb	• Create a Production Folder and Copy an Access File • Open an Access File • Edit a Record • Navigate an Access Form and Add Records • Recognize the Table and Form Connectivity and Delete a Record • Back up and Compact the Database
2. **DATA MANIPULATION: FILTERS AND SORTS (page 96)** **Open:** chap1_ho1-3_traders_soution.accdb (from Exercise 1) **Copy, rename, and backup:** chap1_ho1-3_traders_solution.accdb (additional modifications) chap1_ho2_traders_solution.docx chap1_ho2_traders_solution.accdb	• Use Filter by Selection with an Equal Setting • Use Filter by Selection with a Contains Setting • Use Filter by Form with an Inequity Setting • Sort a Table
3. **INTRODUCTION TO RELATIONSHIPS (page 105)** **Open:** chap1_ho1-3_traders_solution.accdb (from Exercise 2) **Copy, rename, and backup:** chap1_ho1-3_traders_solution.accdb (additional modifications)	• Examine the Relationships Window • Discover that Changes in Table Data Affect Queries • Use Filter by Form with an Inequity Setting and Reapply a Saved Filter • Filter a Report • Remove an Advanced Filter

CASE STUDY

Medical Research—The Lifelong Learning Physicians Association

Today is the first day of your information technology internship appointment with the *Lifelong Learning Physicians Association*. This medical association selected you for the internship because your résumé indicates that you are proficient with Access. Bonnie Clinton, M.D., founded the organization with the purpose of keeping doctors informed about current research and to help physicians identify quali-

Case Study

fied study participants. Dr. Clinton worries that physicians do not inform their patients about study participation opportunities. She expressed further concerns that the physicians in one field, e.g., cardiology, are unfamiliar with research studies conducted in other fields, such as obstetrics.

Because the association is new, you have very little data to manage. However, the system was designed to accommodate additional data. You will need to talk to Dr. Clinton on a regular basis to determine the association's changing information needs. You may need to guide her in this process. Your responsibilities as the association's IT intern include many items.

Your Assignment

- Read the chapter, paying special attention to learning the vocabulary of database software.
- Copy the *chap1_case_physicians.accdb* file to your production folder, rename it **chap1_case_physicians_solution.accdb**, and enable the content.
- Open the Relationships window and examine the relationships among the tables and the fields contained within each of the tables to become acquainted with this database.
- Open the Volunteers table. Add yourself as a study participant by replacing record **22** with your own information. You should invent data about your height, weight, blood pressure, and your cholesterol. Examine the values in the other records and enter a realistic value. Do not change the stored birthday.
- Identify all of the volunteers who might be college freshmen (18- and 19-year-olds). After you identify them, print the table listing their names and addresses. Use a filter by form with an appropriately set date criterion to identify the correctly aged participants.
- Identify all of the physicians participating in a study involving cholesterol management.
- Open the *Studies and Volunteers Report*. Print it.
- Compact and repair the database file.
- Create a backup of the database. Name the backup **chap1_case_physicians_backup.accdb**.

Data and Files Everywhere!

You probably use databases often. Each time you download an MP3 file, you enter a database via the Internet. There you find searchable data identifying files by artist's name, music style, most frequently requested files, first lines, publication companies, and song titles. If you know the name of the song but not the recording artist or record label, you generally can find it. The software supporting the Web site helps you locate the information you need. The server for the Web site provides access to a major database that contains a lot of data about available MP3 files.

You are exposed to other databases on a regular basis. For example, your university uses a database to support the registration process. When you registered for this course, you entered a database. It probably told you how many seats remained but not the names of the other students. In addition, Web-based job and dating boards are based on database software. Organizations rely on data to conduct daily operations, regardless of whether the organization exists as a profit or not-for-profit environment. The organization maintains data about employees, volunteers, customers, activities, and facilities. Every keystroke and mouse click creates data about the organization that needs to be stored, organized, and analyzed. Microsoft Access provides the organizational decision-maker a valuable tool facilitating data retrieval and use.

In this section, you explore Access database objects and work with table views. You also learn the difference between working in storage and memory to understand how changes to database objects are saved. Finally, you practice good file management techniques by backing up, compacting, and repairing databases.

Exploring, Describing, and Navigating Among the Objects in an Access Database

A *field* is a basic entity or data element, such as the name of a book or the telephone number of a publisher.

A *record* is a complete set of all of the data (fields) about one person, place, event, or idea.

A *table* is a collection of records. Every record in a table contains the same fields in the same order.

A *database* consists of one or more tables and the supporting objects used to get data into and out of the tables.

To understand database management effectively and to use Access productively, you should first learn the vocabulary. A *field* is a basic entity, data element, or category, such as book titles or telephone numbers. The field does not necessarily need to contain a value. For example, a field might store fax numbers for a firm's customers. However, some of the customers may not have a fax machine so the Fax field is blank for that record. A *record* is a complete set of all of the data (fields) about one person, place, event, or idea. For example, your name, homework, and test scores constitute your record in your instructor's grade book. A *table*, the foundation of every database, is a collection of related records that contain fields to organize data. If you have used Excel, you will see the similarities between a spreadsheet and an Access table. Each column represents a field, and each row represents a record. Every record in a table contains the same fields in the same order. An instructor's grade book for one class is a table containing records of all students in one structure. A *database* consists of one or more tables and the supporting objects used to get data into and out of the tables.

Prior to the advent of database management software, organizations managed their data manually. They placed papers in file folders and organized the folders in multiple drawer filing cabinets. You can think of the filing cabinet in the manual system as a database. Each drawer full of folders in the filing cabinet corresponds to a table within the database. Figure 1.1 shows a college's database system from before the information age. File drawers (tables) contain student data. Each folder (record) contains facts (fields) about that student. The cabinet also contains drawers (tables) full of data about the faculty and the courses offered. Together, the tables combine to form a database system.

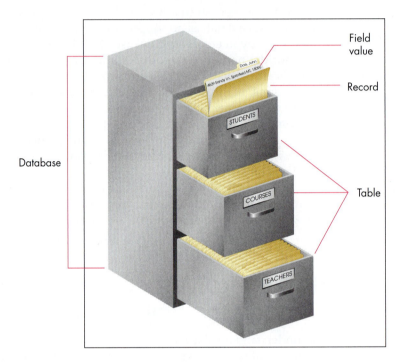

Figure 1.1   Primitive Database

Identify Access Interface Elements

Figure 1.2 shows how Microsoft Access appears onscreen. It contains two open windows—an application window for Microsoft Access and a document (database) window for the open database. Each window has its own title bar and icons. The title bar in the application window contains the name of the application (Microsoft Access) and the Minimize, Maximize (or Restore) icons. The title bar in the document (database) window contains the name of the object that is currently open (Employees table). Should more than one object be open at a time, the top of the document window will display tabs for each open object. The Access application window is maximized; therefore, Restore is visible.

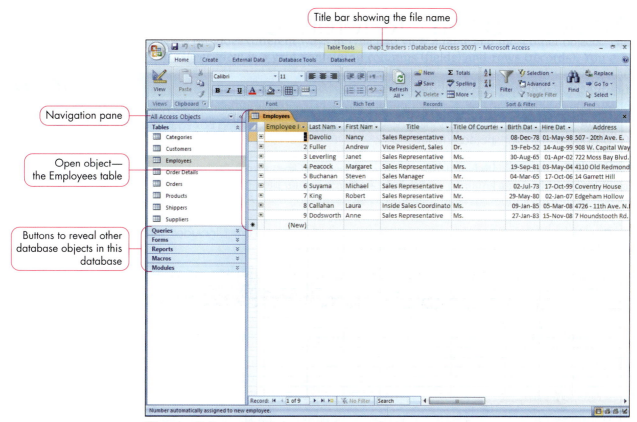

Title bar showing the file name

Navigation pane

Open object— the Employees table

Buttons to reveal other database objects in this database

Figure 1.2 An Access Database

Let's look at an example of a database for an international food distribution company—The Northwind Traders. This firm sells specialty food items to restaurants and food shops around the world. It also purchases the products it sells from diversely located firms. The Northwind Traders Company database contains eight tables: Categories, Customers, Employees, Order Details, Orders, Products, Shippers, and Suppliers. Each table, in turn, consists of multiple records, corresponding to the folders in the file cabinet. The Employees table, for example, contains a record for every employee. Each record in the Employees table contains 17 fields—where data about the employee's education, address, photograph, position, and so on are stored. Occasionally a field does not contain a value for a particular record. One of the employees, Margaret Peacock did not provide a picture. The value of that field is missing. Access provides a placeholder to store the data when it is available. The Suppliers table has a record for each vendor from whom the firm purchases products, just as the Orders table has a record for each order. The real power of Access is derived from a database with multiple tables and the relationships that connect the tables.

The database window displays the various objects in an Access database. An Access *object* stores the basic elements of the database. Access uses six types of objects—tables, queries, forms, reports, macros, and modules. Every database must contain at least one table, and it may contain any, all, or none of the other objects. Each object type is accessed through the appropriate tab within the database window. Because of the interrelationships among objects, you may either view all of the objects of a type in a single place or view all of the related objects in a way that demonstrates their inner-connectivity. You select an object for viewing using the Navigation pane. The Navigation pane on the left side groups related objects.

The Reference page describes the tabs and groups on the Ribbon in Access 2007. You do not need to memorize most of these tabs and groups now. You will learn where things are located as you explore using the features.

An Access *object* contains the basic elements of the database.

A **report** presents database information professionally.

Figure 1.7 displays a report that contains the same information as the query in Figure 1.6. A **report** contains professionally formatted information from underlying tables or queries. Because the report information contains a more enhanced format than a query or table, you place database output in a report to print. Access provides different views for designing, modifying, and running reports. Most Access users use only the Print Preview, Print Layout, and Report views of a report.

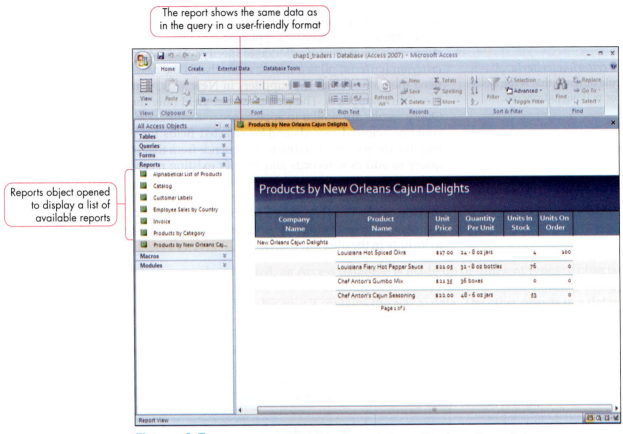

Figure 1.7 Report Displaying the Query Information from Figure 1.6

Understanding the Difference Between Working in Storage and Memory

Access is different from the other Microsoft Office applications. Word, Excel, and PowerPoint all work primarily from memory. In those applications you can easily reverse mistakes by using Undo. You make a change, discover that you dislike it, and click Undo to restore the original. These actions are possible because you work in memory (RAM) most of the time while in the other Microsoft Office applications; changes are not saved automatically to the file immediately after you make the changes. These actions are also possible because, generally, you are the only user of your file. If you work on a group project, you might e-mail the PowerPoint file to the others in the group, but you are the primary owner and user of that file. Access is *different*.

> Access is different from the other Microsoft Office applications.

Access works primarily from storage. When you make a change to a field's content in an Access table (for example, changing a customer's area code), Access saves your changes as soon as you move the insertion point to a different record; you do not need to click Save. You can click Undo to reverse several editing changes (such as changing an area code and a contact name) for a single record **immediately** after making the changes to that record. However, unlike other Office programs that let you continue

Undoing actions, you cannot use Undo to reverse edits to more than the last record you edited or to restore a field if you delete it.

Multiple users can work on the database simultaneously. As long as no two users attempt to interact with the same record at the same time, the system updates as it goes. This also means that any reports extracting the information from the database contain the most up-to-date data. The only time you need to click Save is when you are creating or changing a structural element, such as a table, query, form, or report.

TIP   Save Edits While Keeping a Record Active

When you want to save changes to a record you are editing while staying on the same record, press Shift+Enter. The pencil icon, indicating an editing mode, disappears, indicating that the change is saved.

Be careful to avoid accidentally typing something in a record and pressing Enter. Doing so saves the change, and you can retrieve the original data if you are lucky enough to remember to click Undo immediately before making or editing other records. Because Access is a relational database, several other related objects (queries, reports, or forms) could also be permanently changed. In Access, one file holds everything. All of the objects—tables, forms, queries, and reports—are saved both individually and as part of the Access collection.

TIP   Data Validation

No system, no matter how sophisticated, can produce valid output from invalid input. Thus, good systems are built to anticipate errors in data entry and to reject those errors prior to saving a record. Access will automatically prevent you from adding records with a duplicate primary key or entering invalid data into a numeric or date field. The database developer has the choice whether to require other types of validation, such as requiring the author's name.

Practicing Good File Management

You must exercise methodical and deliberate file management techniques to avoid damaging data. Every time you need to open a file, this book will direct you to copy the file to your production folder and rename the copied file. Name the production folder with **Your Name Access Production**. You would not copy a real database and work in the copy often. However, as you learn, you will probably make mistakes. Following the practice of working in a copied file will facilitate mistake recovery during the learning process.

Further, it matters to which type of media you save your files. Access does not work from some media. Access runs best from a hard or network drive because those drives have sufficient access speed to support the software. Access speed measures the time it takes for the storage device to make the file content available for use. If you work from your own computer, create the production folder in the My Documents folder on the hard drive. Most schools lock their hard drives so that students cannot permanently save files there. If your school provides you with storage space on the school's network, store your production folder there. The advantage to using the network is that the network administration staff backs up files regularly. If you have no storage on the school network, your next best storage option is a thumb drive, also known as USB jump drive, flash drive, Pen drive, or stick drive.

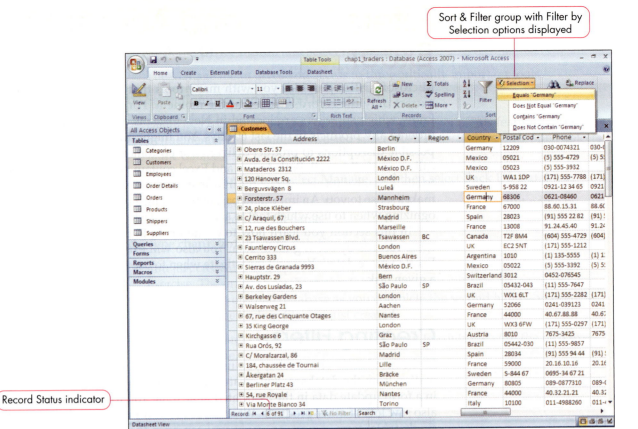

Figure 1.14 Unfiltered Table with Appropriate Sort Options Selected

Figure 1.15 displays a filtered view of the same table in which we see only the customers in Germany. The Navigation bar shows that this is a filtered list and that the filter found 11 records satisfying the criteria. (The Customers table still contains the original 91 records, but only 11 records are visible with the filter applied.)

Toggle to remove filter

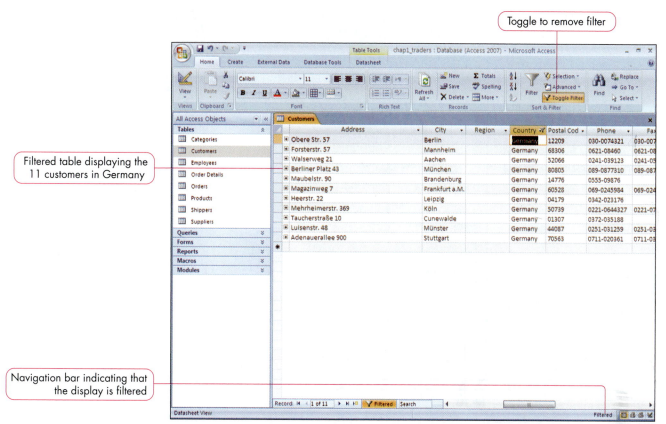

Filtered table displaying the 11 customers in Germany

Navigation bar indicating that the display is filtered

Figure 1.15 Filtered Table with Appropriate Sort Options Selected

TIP Use Quick Keyboard Shortcuts

Look for underlined letters in Access menus. They indicate the letters to use for the keyboard shortcuts. For example, when you click in a field and click the Selection down arrow in the Sort & Filter group, you can click the Equals "London" menu selection or simply type the letter e because the letter E in Equals is underlined, indicating a shortcut key.

Filter by Selection selects only the records that match the pre-selected criteria.

Filter by Form permits selecting criteria from a drop-down list, or applying multiple criteria.

An **inequity** examines a mathematical relationship such as equals, not equals, greater than, less than, greater than or equal to, or less than or equal to.

The easiest way to implement a filter is to click in any cell that contains the value of the desired criterion (such as any cell that contains *Account Rep* in the Title field), then click Filter by Selection in the Sort & Filter group. **Filter by Selection** selects only the records that match the pre-selected criteria.

Figure 1.16 illustrates an alternate and more powerful way to apply a filter. **Filter by Form** permits selecting the criteria from a drop-down list and/or applying multiple criteria simultaneously. However, the real advantage of the Filter by Form command extends beyond these conveniences to two additional capabilities. First, you can specify relationships within a criterion; for example, you can use an inequity setting to select products with an inventory level greater than (or less than) 30. An **inequity** examines a mathematical relationship such as equals, not equals, greater than, less than, greater than or equal to, or less than or equal to. Filter by Selection, on the other hand, requires you to specify criteria equal to an existing value. Figure 1.16 shows the filtered query setup to select Beverages with more than 30 units in stock.

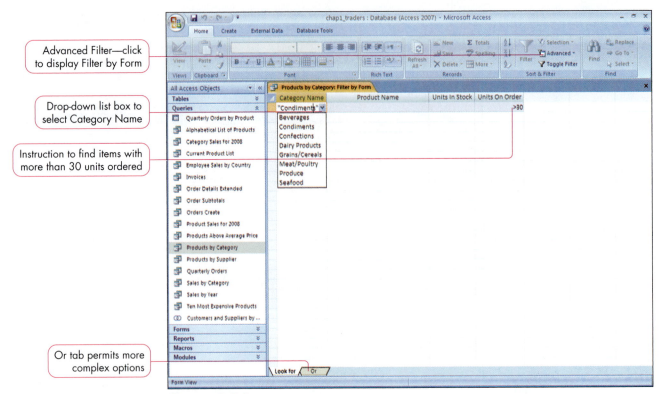

Figure 1.16 Filter by Form Design Grid

Callout labels on figure:
- Advanced Filter—click to display Filter by Form
- Drop-down list box to select Category Name
- Instruction to find items with more than 30 units ordered
- Or tab permits more complex options

A second advantage of the Filter by Form command is that you can specify alternative criteria (such as customers in Germany or orders for over 30 units) by clicking the Or tab. (The latter capability is not implemented in Figure 1.16.) However, the availability of the various filter and sort commands enables you to obtain information from a database quickly and easily without creating a query or report.

Sorting Table Data on One or More Fields

A *sort* lists those records in a specific sequence, such as alphabetically by last name.

Sort Ascending provides an alphabetical list of text data or a small to large list of numeric data.

Sort Descending displays records with the highest value listed first.

You also can change the order of the information by sorting by one or more fields. A *sort* lists those records in a specific sequence, such as alphabetically by last name or by EmployeeID. To sort the table, click in the field on which you want to sequence the records (the LastName field in this example), then click Sort Ascending in the Sort & Filter group on the Home tab. *Sort Ascending* provides an alphabetical list of text data or a small to large list of numeric data. *Sort Descending* is appropriate for numeric fields such as salary, if you want to display the records with the highest value listed first. Figure 1.17 shows the Customers table sorted in alphabetical order by country. You may apply both filters and sorts to table or query information to select and order the data in the way that you need to make decisions.

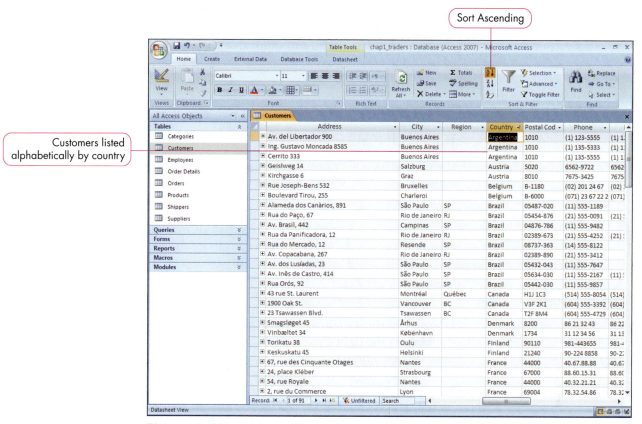

Sort Ascending

Customers listed alphabetically by country

Figure 1.17 Customers Table Sorted by Country

The operations can be done in any order; that is, you can filter a table to show only selected records, then you can sort the filtered table to display the records in a different order. Conversely, you can sort a table and then apply a filter. It does not matter which operation is performed first, and indeed, you can go back and forth between the two. You can also filter the table further, by applying a second (or third) criterion; for example, click in a cell containing *USA* and apply a Filter by Selection. Then click in a record for Oregon (OR) and apply a Filter by Selection a second time to display the customers from Oregon. You also can click Toggle Filter at any time to display all of the records in the table. Filters are a temporary method for examining subsets of data. If you close the filtered table or query and reopen it, all of the records display.

TIP The Sort or Filter—Which is First?

It doesn't matter whether you sort a table and then apply a filter, or filter first and then sort. The operations are cumulative. Thus, after you sort a table, any subsequent display of filtered records for that table will be in the specified sequence. Alternatively, you can apply a filter and then sort the filtered table by clicking in the desired field and clicking the appropriate sort command. Remember, too, that all filter commands are cumulative, and hence you must remove the filter to see the original table.

You may be familiar with applying a filter, sorting data, or designing a form using Excel. The fact is, Excel can accomplish all of these activities. You need to examine your data needs and think about what your future data requirements may be to decide whether to use Access or Excel.

Knowing When to Use Access or Excel to Manage Data

If you have the ability to control data and turn it into useful information, you possess a marketable skill. It does not matter whether you are planning to become a social worker, a teacher, an engineer, an entrepreneur, a radiologist, a marketer, a day care worker, a musician, or an accountant. You will need to collect, store, maintain, manage, and protect data as well as convert it into information used to make strategic decisions. A widely used program that you probably already know is Excel. This course will help you become familiar with Access. You can accomplish many of the same things in either software. Although the two packages have much in common, they each have advantages. So, how do you choose whether to use Access or Excel?

> If you have the ability to control data and turn it into useful information, you possess a marketable skill.

Making the right choice is critical if you want to find and update your information with maximum performance and accuracy. Ideally, your data needs and the type and amount of data used will determine how to pick the program that will work best. Sometimes organizations use Access when they probably would be better served with Excel and vice-versa. The answer to the question of which to use may depend on who you ask. An accountant probably will use Excel. The information technology professional probably will use a more sophisticated database software like Oracle, but not Access. The middle manager in the marketing or manufacturing department will probably use Access. The question remains.

Select the Software to Use

A contacts list is an example of flat data. Each column of data (names, addresses, and phone numbers) is logically related to the others. If you can store your data logically in a single table or worksheet, then do. Update your data in the same type of file. Data contained in a single page or sheet (not multiple) are called *flat* or *non-relational data*. You would never store your friend's last name on a different sheet from the sheet containing the friend's cell phone number.

> Data contained in a single page or sheet (not multiple) are called *flat* or *non-relational data*.

Suppose you had a spreadsheet of club members' names and contact information. Your club decides to sell cookies as a fundraiser. You might create a new worksheet listing how many boxes of which type of cookie each member picked up to sell. Your third worksheet might show how much money each member has turned in from the cookie sales. These data are different. They are not flat. Can you imagine needing to know someone's phone number or how many cookie boxes he or she promised to sell while looking at the worksheet of data about how much money has been turned in? These data are multi-dimensional and need to be stored in more than one worksheet or table. This describes relational data. Each table holds a particular type of data (number of boxes collected, contact information, funds turned in). Relational data are best stored in Access. In this example, you would create a database with three tables. You need to adhere to the following rules about assigning data to the appropriate table.

Assign table data so that each table:

- Represents only a single subject
- Has a field(s) that uniquely identifies each record
- Does not contain duplicate fields
- Has no repetition of the same type of value
- Has no fields belonging in other tables

As the quantity and complexity of data increase, the need to organize it efficiently also increases. Access affords better data organization than Excel. Access accomplishes the organization through a system of linkages among the tables. Each record (row) should be designated with a primary key—a unique identifier that sets it apart from all of the other records in the table. The primary key might be an account number, a student identification number, or an employee access code. All data in Excel have a unique identifier—the cell address. In life, you have a Social Security Number. It's the best unique identifier you have. Ever notice how, when at the doctor's office or applying for college admission, you are asked for your Social Security Number as well as your name? Your record in its database system probably uses your Social Security Number as a unique identifier.

You still need to answer the question of when to use Access and when to use Excel.

Use Access

You should use Access to manage data when you:

- Require a relational database (multiple tables or multi-dimensional tables) to store your data or anticipate adding more tables in the future.

  For example, you may set your club membership contact list in either software, but if you believe that you also will need to keep track of the cookie sales and fund collection, use Access.

- Have a large amount of data.

- Rely on external databases to derive and analyze the data you need.

  If frequently you need to have Excel exchange data to or from Access, use Access. Even though the programs are compatible, it makes sense to work in Access to minimize compatibility issues.

- Need to maintain constant connectivity to a large external database, such as one built with Microsoft SQL Server or your organization's Enterprise Resource Planning system.

- Need to regroup data from different tables in a single place through complex queries.

  You might need to create output showing how many boxes of cookies each club member picked up and how much money they turned in along with the club member's name and phone number.

- Have many people working in the database and need strong options to update the data.

  For example, five different clerks at an auto parts store might wait on five different customers. Each clerk connects to the inventory table to find out if the needed part is in stock and where in the warehouse it is located. When the customer says, "Yes, I want that" the inventory list is instantly updated and that product is no longer available to be purchased by the other four customers.

Use Excel

You should use Excel to manage data when you:

- Require a flat or non-relational view of your data (you do not need a relational database with multiple tables).

  This idea is especially true if that data is mostly numeric—for example, if you need to maintain an expense statement.

- Want to run primarily calculations and statistical comparisons on your data.

- Know your dataset is manageable in size (no more than 15,000 rows).

  In the next exercise you will create and apply filters, perform sorts, and develop skills to customize the data presentation to answer your questions.

The Relational Database

In the previous section you read that you should use Access when you have multi-dimensional data. Access derives power from multiple tables and the relationships among those tables. A *relational database management system* is one in which data are grouped into similar collections called tables, and the relationships between tables are formed by using a common field. The design of a relational database system is illustrated in Figure 1.22. The power of a relational database lies in the software's ability to organize data and combine items in different ways to obtain a complete picture of the events the data describe. Good database design connects the data in different tables through a system of linkages. These links are the relationships that give relational databases the name. Look at Figure 1.1. The student record (folder) contains information about the student, but also contains cross-references to data stored in other cabinet drawers, such as the advisor's name or a list of courses completed. If you need to know the advisor's phone number, you can open the faculty drawer, find the advisor's record, and then locate the field containing the phone number. The cross-reference from the student file to the faculty file illustrates how a relationship works in a database. Figure 1.22 displays the cross-references between the tables as a series of lines connecting the common fields. When the database is set up properly, the users of the data can be confident that if they search a specific customer identification number, they will be given accurate information about that customer's order history and payment balances, and his/her product or shipping preferences.

In this section, you will explore the relationships among tables, learn about the power of relational integrity, and discover how the software protects the organization's data.

A *relational database management system* is one in which data are grouped into similar collections, called tables, and the relationships between tables are formed by using a common field.

(The power of a relational database lies in the software's ability to organize data and combine items in different ways to obtain a complete picture of the events the data describe.)

Using the Relationship Window

The relationship (the lines between the tables in Figure 1.22) is like a piece of electronic string that travels throughout the database, searching every record of every table until it finds the data satisfying the user's request. Once identified, the fields and records of interest will be tied to the end of the string, pulled through the computer and reassembled in a way that makes the data easy to understand. The first end of the string was created when the primary key was established in the Customers table. The primary key is a unique identifier for each table record. The other end of the string will be tied to a field in a different table. If you examine Figure 1.22, you will see that the CustomerID is a foreign field in the Orders table. A *foreign key* is a field in one table that also is stored in a different table as a primary key. Each value of the CustomerID can occur only once in the Customers table because it is a primary key. However, the CustomerID may appear multiple times in the Orders table because one customer may make many different purchases. The CustomerID field is a foreign key in the Orders table but the primary key in the Customers table.

A *foreign key* is a field in one table that also is stored in a different table as a primary key.

Examine Referential Integrity

The relationships connecting the tables will be created using an Access feature that uses referential integrity. Integrity means truthful or reliable. When *referential integrity* is enforced, the user can trust the "threads" running through the database and "tying" related items together. The sales manager can use the database to find the names and phone numbers of all the customers who have ordered Teatime Chocolate Biscuits (a specific product). Because referential integrity has been enforced, it will not matter that the order information is in a different table from the customer data. The invisible threads will keep the information accurately connected. The threads also provide a method of ensuring data accuracy. You cannot enter a record in the Orders table that references a ProductID or a CustomerID that does not exist elsewhere in the system. Nor can you easily delete a record in one table if it has related records in related tables.

Referential integrity is the set of rules that ensure that data stored in related tables remain consistent as the data are updated.

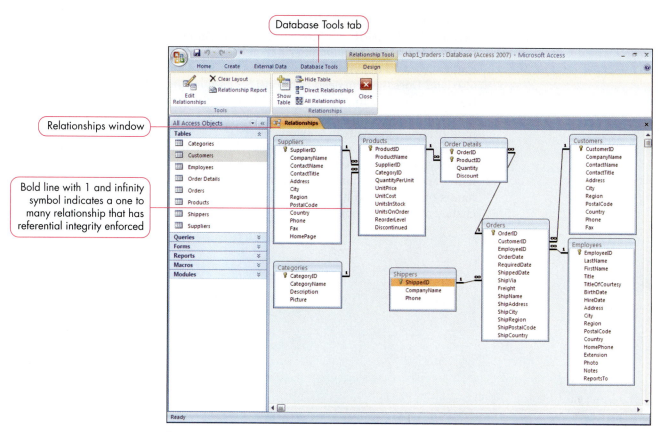

Figure 1.22 The Relationships Window Displaying Table Connections

If this were a real organization's data system, the files would be much, much larger and the data more sophisticated. When learning database skills, you should start with smaller, more manageable files. The same design principles apply regardless of the database size. A small file gives you the ability to check the tables and see if your results are correct. Even though the data amounts are small, you need to develop the work practices needed to manage large amounts of data. With only a handful of records, you can easily count the number of employees at the Washington state office. In addition to learning how to accomplish a task, you also should begin to learn to anticipate the computer's response to an instruction. As you work, ask yourself what the anticipated results should be and then verify. When you become skilled at anticipating output correctly, you are surprised less often.

> As you work, ask yourself what the anticipated results should be and then verify. When you become skilled at anticipating output correctly, you are surprised less often.

Understanding Relational Power

In the previous section you read that you should use Access when you have multidimensional data. Access derives power from multiple tables and the relationships between those tables. This type of database is known as a relational database and is illustrated in Figure 1.22. This figure describes the database structure. Examine some of the connections. The EmployeeID is a foreign field in the Orders table. For example, you can produce a document displaying the history of each order a customer had placed and the employee's name (from the Employees table) that entered the order. The Orders table references the Order Details table where the OrderID is a foreign field. The ProductID relates to the Products table (where it is the primary key). The CategoryID is the primary key in the Categories table, but shows up as a foreign field in the Products table. The table connections, even when more than one table is involved, provide the decision-maker power. This feature gives the manager the ability to find out sales by category. How many different beverages were shipped last week? What was the total revenue generated from seafood orders last year?

Suppose a customer called to complain that his orders were arriving late. Because the ShipperID is a foreign field in the Orders table, you could look up which shipper delivered that customer's merchandise and then find out what other customers received deliveries from that shipper the same month. Are the other orders also late? Does the firm need to reconsider its shipping options? The design of a relational database enables us to extract information from multiple tables in a single query or report. Equally important, it simplifies the way data are changed in that modifications are made in only one place.

In the previous hands-on exercises, you have made modifications to table data. You created a new product, you changed an employee and customer name to your name, and you sorted data. You will trace through some of those changes in the next hands-on exercise to help you understand the power of relationships and how a change made to one object travels throughout the database file structure.

Hands-On Exercises

3 | Introduction to Relationships

Skills covered: 1. Examine the Relationships Window **2.** Discover that Changes in Table Data Affect Queries **3.** Use Filter by Form with an Inequity Setting and Reapply a Saved Filter **4.** Filter a Report **5.** Remove an Advanced Filter

Step 1 **Examine the** **Relationships Window**	Refer to Figure 1.23 as you complete Step 1. **a.** Open the *chap1_ho1-3_traders_solution* file if necessary, click **Options** on the *security warning* toolbar, click the **Enable this content option** in the Microsoft Office Security Options dialog box, and click **OK**.

TROUBLESHOOTING: If you create unrecoverable errors while completing this hands-on exercise, you can delete the *chap1_ho1-3_traders_solution* file, copy the *chap1_ho2_traders_solution* database you created at the end of the second hands-on exercise, and open the copy of the backup database to start the third hands-on exercise again.

b. Click the **Database Tools tab** and click **Relationships** in the Show/Hide group.

Examine the relationships that connect the various tables. For example, the Products table is connected to the Suppliers, Categories, and Order Details tables.

c. Click **Show Table**.

The Show Table dialog box opens. It tells you that there are eight available tables in the database. If you look in the Relationship window, you will see that all eight tables are in the relationship diagram.

d. Click the **Queries tab** in the Show Table dialog box.

You could add all of the queries to the Relationships window. Things might become cluttered, but you could tell at a glance where the queries get their information.

e. Close the Show Table dialog box.

f. Click the **down arrow** in the All Access Objects bar of the Navigation pane.

g. Click **Tables and Related Views**.

You can now see not only the tables, but also the queries, forms, and reports that connect to the table data. If a query is sourced on more than one table, it will appear multiple times in the Navigation pane. This view provides an alternate method of viewing the relationships connecting the tables.

h. Close the Relationships window. Save the changes.

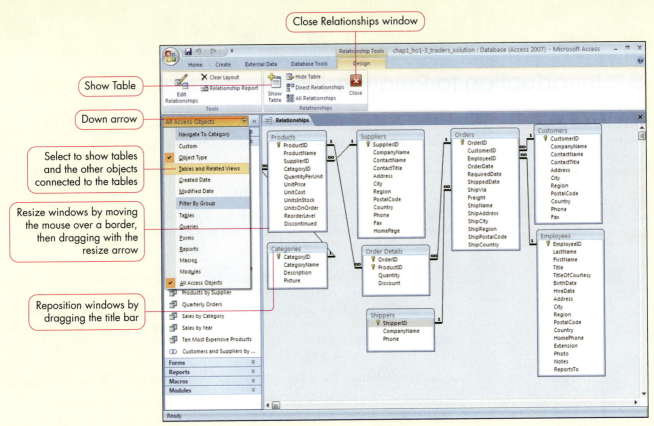

Close Relationships window

Show Table

Down arrow

Select to show tables and the other objects connected to the tables

Resize windows by moving the mouse over a border, then dragging with the resize arrow

Reposition windows by dragging the title bar

Figure 1.23 The Relationships Window Displaying the Northwind Table Relationships

Step 2

Discover that Changes in Table Data Affect Queries

Refer to Figure 1.24 as you complete Step 2.

a. Scroll in the Navigation pane until you see the *Products table and Related Objects*. Locate and double-click the **Order Details Extended query**.

b. Examine the icons on the left edge of the Navigation pane. Figure 1.24 identifies the object type for each of the objects.

c. Find an occurrence of *your last name* anywhere in the query (record 7 should show your name) and click it to make it active.

The query contains your name because in Hands-On Exercise 1 you replaced Margaret Peacock's name in the Employees table with your name. The Employees table is related to the Orders table, the Orders table to the Order Details table, and the Order Details table to the Products table. Therefore, any change you make to the Employees table is carried throughout the database via the relationships.

d. Click **Filter by Selection** in the Sort & Filter group. Select **Equals "YourName"** from the selection menu.

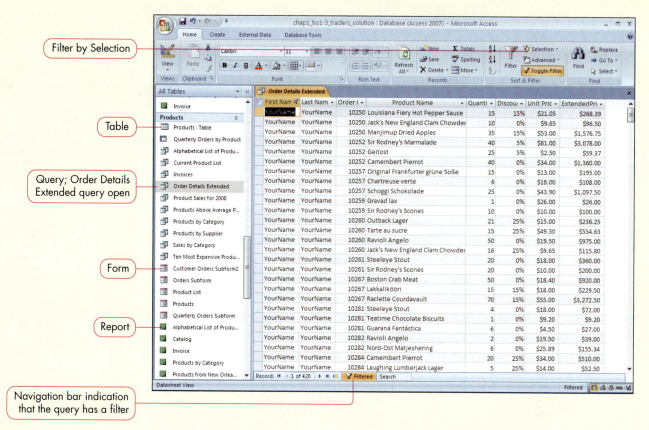

Filter by Selection

Table

Query; Order Details
Extended query open

Form

Report

Navigation bar indication
that the query has a filter

Figure 1.24 Filtered Query Results

Step 3
Use Filter by Form with an Inequity Setting and Reapply a Saved Filter

Refer to Figure 1.25 as you complete Step 3.

a. Click **Advanced Filter options**.

b. Select **Filter By Form** from the drop-down list.

   Because you already applied a filter to these data, the Filter By Form design sheet opens with one criterion already filled in. Your name displays in the selection box under the Last Name field.

c. Scroll right (or press **Tab**) until the Extended Price field is visible. Click the insertion point in the **first row** under the Extended Price field.

d. Type **>2000**.

   The Extended Price field shows the purchased amount for each item ordered. If an item sold for $15 and a customer ordered 10, the Extended Price would display $150.

e. Click **Toggle Filter** in the Sort & Filter group. Examine the filtered results.

   Your inequity instruction, >2000, identified the items ordered where the extended price exceeded $2,000.

f. Press **Ctrl+S** to save the query. Close the query by clicking the X in the object window.

g. Open the **Order Details Extended query**.

   The filter disengages when you close and reopen the object. However, your filtering directions have been stored with the query design. You may reapply the filter at any time by clicking the Toggle Filter command.

h. Click **Toggle Filter** in the Sort & Filter group.

i. Compare your work to Figure 1.25. If it is correct, close the query.

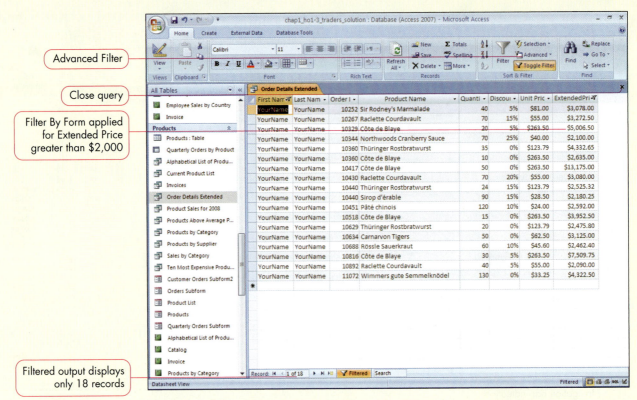

Advanced Filter

Close query

Filter By Form applied for Extended Price greater than $2,000

Filtered output displays only 18 records

Figure 1.25 Filtered Query Results after Limiting Output to Extended Prices over $2,000

Step 4
Filter a Report

Refer to Figure 1.26 as you complete Step 4.

a. Open the **Products by Category report** located in the Navigation pane under the Products group. You may need to scroll down to locate it.

The report should open in Print Preview with a gray stripe highlighting the report title. The Print Preview displays the report exactly as it will print. This report was formatted to display in three columns.

TROUBLESHOOTING: If you do not see the gray stripe and three columns, you probably opened the wrong object. The database also contains a Product by Category query. It is the source for the Products by Category report. Make sure you open the report (shown with the green report icon) and not the query. Close the query and open the report.

b. Examine the Confections category products. You should see **Your Name Pecan Pie**.

You created this product by entering data in a form in Hands-On Exercise 1. You later discovered that changes made to a form affect the related table. Now you see that other related objects also change when the source data changes.

c. Right-click the **gold report tab**. Select **Report View** from the shortcut menu.

The Report view displays the information a little differently. It no longer shows three columns. If you clicked the Print command while in Report view, the columns would print even though you do not see them. The Report view permits limited data interaction (for example, filtering).

d. Scroll down in the report until you see the title *Category: Confections*. **Right-click** the word **Confections** in the title. Select **Equals "Confections"** from the shortcut menu.

Right-clicking a selected data value in an Access table, query, form, or report activates a shortcut to a Filter by Selection menu. Alternatively you can click the selected value, in this case, Confections, and then click the Filter by Selection command in the Sort & Filter group.

e. Right-click the **gold report tab**. Select **Print Preview** from the shortcut menu.

You need to print this report. Always view your reports in Print Preview prior to printing.

f. Click the **Office Button**, position the mouse pointer over **Print**, and then select **Quick Print** to produce a printed copy of the filtered report. Click **OK**.

The Quick Print command sends your work to the default printer as soon as you click it. You can use this safely when you have already viewed your work in Print Preview.

g. Save and close the report.

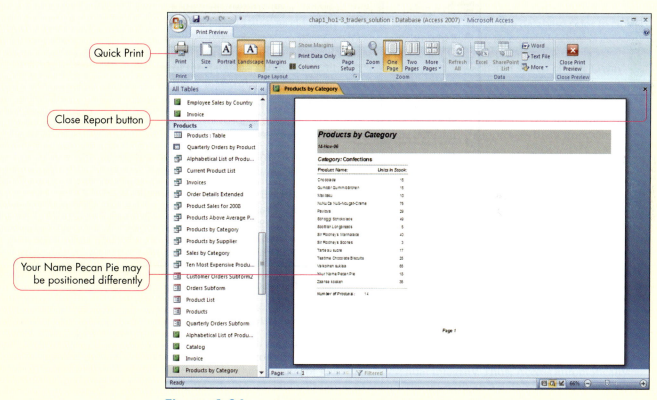

Figure 1.26 Filtered Report Results

Refer to Figure 1.27 as you complete Step 5.

Step 5
Remove an Advanced Filter

a. Open the **Order Details Extended query**.

All 2,155 records should display in the query. You have unfiltered the data. However the filter still exists.

i. Type **4** in the *Product ID box* and **2** in *Quantity*. In the next row, type **6** and **1** for *Product ID* and *Quantity*. The Product IDs will convert to P0004 and P0006. Close the form, saving changes if requested.

j. Open the **Order Details Report**. Scroll down to verify that your name appears both as a customer and as a sales rep. Right-click **your name** in the SalesRep field and select **Equals "Your Name"** from the shortcut menu. Right click **Miami** in the City field and select **Equals "Miami"** from the shortcut menu.

k. Click the **Office Button**, position the mouse pointer over **Print**, and select **Print Preview**. Click **Print**.

l. Click the **Office Button**, select **Manage**, and then select **Compact and Repair Database**.

m. Click the **Office Button**, select **Manage**, and then select **Back Up Database**. Use the default backup filename. Close the file.

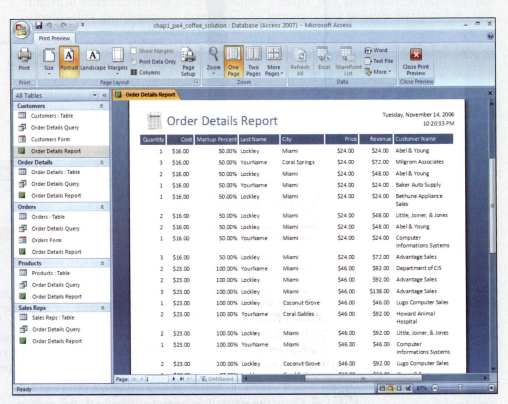

Figure 1.31 Report Showing Changes Made to Forms

Your little sister lives to play soccer. She told her coach that you have become a computer expert. Coach (who is also the league director) called you to ask for help with the Access database file containing all of the league information. You agreed, and he promptly delivered a disc containing a copy of the league's database. The file contains information on the players, the coaches, and the teams. Players are classified by skill and experience level, with the best players described as "A." The Coaches table classifies coaching status as level 1 (head coaches) or 2 (assistant coaches). Coach asks that you add new players to the database and then identify all of the players not yet assigned to teams. He also needs you to identify the teams without coaches, the unassigned coaches, and asks that you assign each team a head and an assistant coach. Finally, Coach convinces you to volunteer as a coach in the league. Verify your work by looking at Figure 1.32.

a. Locate the file named *chap1_mid1_soccer.accdb*, copy it to your working folder, and rename it **chap1_mid1_soccer_solution.accdb**. Open the file and enable the content.

b. Open the Relationships window and examine the tables, the relationships, and the fields located in each table. Close the Relationships window.

c. Examine all of the objects in the database and think about the work Coach asked you to do. Identify which objects will assist you in accomplishing the assigned tasks.

d. Open the **Players form** and create a new record. Use your name, but you may invent the data about your address and phone. You are classified as an "A" player. Print the form containing your record. Close the form.

e. Open the **Coaches table**. Replace record 13 with **your instructor's name**. Add **yourself** as a new record. You are a *coach status* **1**.

f. Identify the players not assigned to teams. Assign each player to a team while balancing skill levels. (You would not want one team in the league to have all of the "A" skill level players because they would always win.)

g. Identify the teams without coaches and the coaches not assigned to teams. Assign a head coach and an assistant coach to each team. You may need to assign a person with head coaching qualifications to an assistant position. If you do, change his or her *status* to **2**.

h. After you assign all of the players and coaches to teams, open and print the **Master Coaching List report**.

i. After you assign all of the players and coaches to teams, open and print the **Team Rosters report**. Close the database.

...continued on Next Page

Customer's Last Name—Text

Customer's First Name—Text

Customer's Identification Number—Either text or number

Address—Text

City—Text

State—Text

Postal Code—Number

Phone—Text

Branch Identification—Either text or number

Branch Manager's Name—Text

Branch Manager's Start Date—Number date formatted

Branch Location—Text

Account Number—Either text or number

Balance—Number formatted as currency

Figure 2.1 Data Needed for a Bank Database

Figure 2.1 reflects the results of a careful design process based on six essential guidelines:

1. Include the necessary data.

2. Design for the next 100 years.

3. Design in compliance with Sarbanes Oxley.

4. Design in compliance with PNPI Regulations.

5. Store data in its smallest parts.

6. Avoid calculated fields in table data.

7. Design to accommodate date arithmetic.

The following paragraphs discuss these guidelines. As you proceed through the text, you will begin developing the experience necessary to design your own systems. Design is an important skill. You also must understand how to design a database and its tables to use Access effectively.

Include the Necessary Data

> . . . ask yourself what information will be expected from the system, and then determine the data required to produce that information.

The best way to determine what data are necessary is to create a rough draft of the reports you will need, and then design tables that contain the fields necessary to create those reports. In other words, ask yourself what information will be expected from the system, and then determine the data required to produce that information. Consider, for example, the type of information that can and cannot be produced from the table in Figure 2.1:

• You can determine which branch a customer uses. You cannot, however, tell the customer with multiple accounts at different locations what the total balance of all accounts might be.

- You can calculate a total of all account balances by adding individual account balances together. You could also calculate the sum of all deposits at a branch. You cannot tell when a deposit was made because this small exercise does not store that data.

- You can determine who manages a particular branch and which accounts are located there. You cannot determine how long the customer has banked with the branch because the date that he or she opened the account is not in the table.

Whether these omissions are important depends on the objectives of the system. Of course, the data stored in a real bank's database is far more complex and much larger than the data you will use. This case has been simplified.

Design for the Next 100 Years

A fundamental law of information technology states that systems evolve continually and that information requirements change. Try to anticipate the future needs of the system, and then build in the flexibility to satisfy those demands. Include the necessary data at the outset, and be sure that the field sizes are large enough to accommodate future expansion. The *field size property* defines how many characters to reserve for a specific field.

The *field size property* defines how much space to reserve for each field.

When you include all possible elements of data that anyone might ever need, you drive up the cost of the database. Each element costs employee time to enter and maintain the data and consumes storage space. Computers have a finite amount of space. Good database design must balance the current and future needs of the system against the cost of recording and storing unnecessary data elements. Even with using data warehouses, the amount of data that we can store is limited.

(Good database design must balance the current and future needs of the system against the cost of recording and storing unnecessary data elements.)

Suppose you are designing a database for your college. You would need to include students' on-campus and permanent addresses. It might be useful for someone to know other places a student might have lived or even visited during their lives. A worker in the Student Life office could help an international student connect with someone who used to live in or at least visited the international student's homeland. A student who had moved often or traveled extensively might need an extra page on his or her application form. Completing the application might take so long that the student might apply to a different college. A worker in the admissions office would need extra time to enter all the places of residence and travel into the database. The school's database file would grow and require additional storage space on the university computer system. The benefits provided to the international student from connecting him to someone who had been in his country may not justify the cost of entering, maintaining, and storing the additional data.

The data will prove useful only if they are accurate. You need to anticipate possible errors a data entry operator might commit. Access provides tools to protect data from user error. A *validation rule* restricts data entry in a field to ensure the correct type of data is entered or that the data does not violate other enforced properties, such as exceed a size limitation. The validation rule checks the authenticity of the data entered when the user exits the field. If the data entry violates the validation rule, an error message appears and prevents the invalid data from being stored in the field.

A *validation rule* checks the authenticity of the data entered in a field.

Design in Compliance with Sarbanes Oxley

Following the financial and accounting scandals involving Enron and World Com in 2002, the U.S. Congress passed the *Sarbanes Oxley Act (SOX)*. Its intent is to protect the general public and companies' shareholders against fraudulent practices and accounting errors. The Securities and Exchange Commission (SEC) enforces the act. Although primarily focused on the accounting practices followed by publicly traded companies, SOX permeates corporate Information Technology policies and practices. The act requires that all business records, including electronic messages, be saved for a period of five years and be made available to the SEC on request. Penalties for

Sarbanes Oxley Act (SOX) protects the general public and companies' shareholders against fraudulent practices and accounting errors.

non-compliance include fines, imprisonment, or both. The IT department faces the challenge of archiving all the required information in a cost-effective and efficient way.

Design in Compliance with PNPI Regulations

Federal laws and regulations govern the safeguarding of personal, non-public information (*PNPI*), such as Social Security Numbers (SSNs), credit or bank account numbers, medical or educational records, or other sensitive, confidential or protected data (i.e., grades used in context with personally identifiable information such as name, address, or other easily traceable identifiers). Organizations must store your personal information in computer systems. For example, without your Social Security Number, the financial aid office cannot release scholarship money to pay your tuition. Your employer cannot cut a paycheck without knowing your Social Security Number. Your doctor cannot tell the student health service at your school whether you have been immunized against the measles without your written permission. The data must be stored with protected and restricted access. Congress has passed several laws to protect you from identity theft or other misuse of your private, personal information. The most important of these laws include the following:

- Family Educational Rights and Privacy Act (FERPA) [educational records]
- Gramm-Leach-Bliley Act (GLBA) [financial institution and customer data]
- Health Insurance Portability and Accountability Act (HIPAA) [health information]

Store Data in Their Smallest Parts

The design in Figure 2.1 divides a customer's name into two fields (first and last name) to reference each field individually. You might think it easier to use a single field consisting of both the first and last name, but that approach is inadequate. Consider this list in which the customer's name is stored as a single field:

- Allison Foster
- Brit Reback
- Carrie Graber
- Danielle Ferrarro
- Evelyn Adams
- Frances Coulter

The first problem in this approach is lack of flexibility: You could not easily create a salutation of the form *Dear Allison* or *Dear Ms. Foster* because the first and last names are not accessible individually. In actuality you could write a procedure to divide the name field in two, but that is beyond the capability of the Access novice.

A second difficulty is that the list of customers cannot be put into alphabetical order by last name very easily because the last name begins in the middle of the field. The names are already alphabetized by first name because sorting always begins with the left position in a field. Thus the "A" in Allison comes before the "B" in Brit, and so on. The proper way to sort the data is on the last name, which can be done more efficiently if the last name is stored as a separate field.

Think of how an address might be used. The city, state, and postal code should always be stored as separate fields. Any type of mass mailing requires you to sort on postal codes to take advantage of bulk mail. Other applications may require you to select records from a particular state or postal code, which can be done more efficiently if you store the data as separate fields. Often database users enter the postal code, and the database automatically retrieves the city and state information. You may need to direct a mailing to only a neighborhood or to a single street. The guideline is simple: Store data in their smallest parts.

Avoid Calculated Fields in Table Data

A *calculated field* is a field that derives its value from a formula that references one or more existing fields.

A *calculated field* produces a value from an expression—a formula or function that references an existing field or combination of fields. Although the information derived from calculations can be incredibly valuable to the decision maker, it is useful only at the moment the calculation is made. It makes no sense to store outdated data when recalculating; it will provide the decision maker with fresh, accurate information. Calculated fields should not be stored in a table because they are subject to change and waste space.

The total account balance for a customer with multiple accounts is an example of a calculated field because it is computed by adding the balances in all of the customer's accounts together. It is unnecessary to store the calculated sum of account balances in the Account table, because the table contains the fields on which the sum is based. In other words, Access is able to calculate the sum from these fields whenever it is needed, which is much more efficient than doing it manually.

Design to Accommodate Date Arithmetic

A *constant* is an unchanging value, like a birth date.

Date arithmetic is the process of subtracting one date from another.

A *date/time field* is a field that facilitates calculations for dates and times.

A person's age and date of birth provide equivalent information, as one is calculated from the other. It might seem easier, therefore, to store the age rather than the birth date to avoid the calculation. That would be a mistake because age changes continually and needs to be updated continually, but the date of birth remains *constant*—an unchanging value. Similar reasoning applies to an employee's length of service versus date of hire. Like Excel, Access stores all dates as a serial integer. You can use *date arithmetic* to subtract one date from another to find out the number of days, months, or years that have lapsed between them. Access provides a special data definition for *date/time fields* to facilitate calculations.

Design Multiple Tables

Data redundancy occurs when unnecessary duplicate information exists in a database.

After listing all of the data items that you want to include in the database, you need to group them into similar items. Group the customer information into one table, the branch information into another, and the account information into a third table. A well-designed database provides a means of recombining the data when needed. When the design is sound, the **referential integrity** rules ensure that consistent data is stored in a related table. For example, the Customers and Account tables are linked by relationship. Referential integrity ensures that only valid customer IDs that exist in the Customers table are used in the Account table; it prevents you from entering an invalid customer ID in the Account table.

Avoid *data redundancy*, which is the unnecessary inclusion of duplicate data among tables. You should never store duplicate information in multiple tables in a database. The information about a customer's address should only exist in a single table, the Customers table. It would be poor database design to also include the customer's address in the Account table. When duplicate information exists in a database, errors may result. Suppose the address data were stored in both the Customers and Account tables. You need to anticipate the consequences that may result when a customer moves. A likely outcome would be that the address would be updated in one but not both tables. The result would be unreliable data. Depending on which table served as the source for the output, either the new or the old address might be provided to the manager requesting the information. It is a much stronger design to have the address stored in only one table but tied to the rest of the database through the power of the relationships. See Figure 2.2.

e. Double-click the **Branch table** in the Navigation Pane to open the table. Check the start dates.

You did not save any changes you made; you closed the table without saving changes. The dates are correct because Access works from storage, not memory.

f. Click the **Office Button**, position the mouse pointer over **Print**, and then select **Quick Print**.

Most users do not print Access table data. Tables store and organize data and rarely generate output. People do not spend time formatting table data. Check with your instructor to see if you should submit a printed Branch table for feedback.

g. Click the **Office Button**, select **Manage**, and then select **Back Up Database**. Type **chap2_ho1_safebank_solution** as the filename and then click **Save**.

You just created a backup of the database after completing the first hands-on exercise. The original database *chap2_ho1-3_safebank_solution* remains onscreen. If you ruin the original database as you complete the second hands-on exercise, you can use the backup file you just created and rework the second exercise.

h. Close the file and exit Access if you do not want to continue with the next exercise at this time.

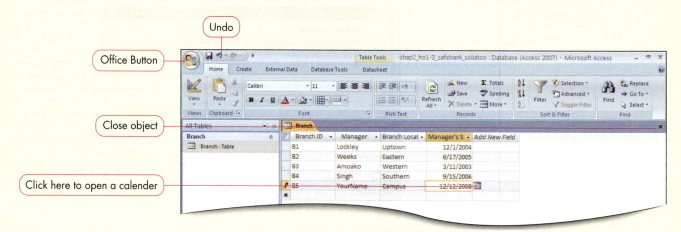

Figure 2.11 Calendar Facilitates Data Entry

Multiple Table Database

Earlier you designed a database and combined similar data items into groupings called tables. You have completed the first table in the database, the Branch table. If you re-examine your design notes and Figure 2.2, recall that you planned for two additional tables in the Safebank database. The power of a relational database lies in its ability to organize and combine data in different ways to obtain a complete picture of the events the data describe. Good database design connects the data in different tables through links. These links are the relationships that give relational databases the name. In your Safebank database one customer can have many accounts or can bank at any of the bank locations. That is, the customer's ID may be listed for many account numbers in the Accounts table, but the customer's ID is listed only one time in the Customers table. When the database is set up properly, database users can be confident that if they search for a specific customer identification number, they will be given accurate information about that customer's account balances, address, or branch preferences.

In this section, you learn about table relationships, referential integrity, indexing, and importing data from Excel.

Understanding Table Relationships

The relationship is like a piece of electronic string that travels throughout the database, searching every record of every table until it finds the events of interest. Once identified, the fields and records of interest will be tied to the end of the string, pulled through the computer, and reassembled in a way that makes the data easy to understand. The first end of the string was created when the primary key was established in the Branch table. The primary key is a unique identifier for each table record. The other end of the string ties to a field in a different table. You will include the Branch ID as a foreign field in the Accounts table. A foreign key is a field in one table that is also stored in a different table as a primary key. Each value of the Branch ID (BID) can occur only once in the Branch table because it is a primary key. However, the BID may appear multiple times in the account table because many different accounts are at the same branch.

Establish Referential Integrity

The relationships will be created using an Access feature that enforces referential integrity. Integrity means truthful or reliable. When referential integrity is enforced, the user can trust the threads running through the database and tying related items together. The Campus branch manager can use the database to find the names and phone numbers of all the customers with accounts at the Campus branch. Because referential integrity has been enforced, it will not matter that the branch information is in a different table from the customer data. The invisible threads keep the information accurately connected. Managers need organized and dependable data upon which they base decisions. The threads also provide a method of ensuring data accuracy. You cannot enter a record in the Account table that references a Branch ID or a Customer ID that does not exist in the system. Nor can you delete a record in one table if it has related records in other tables.

(As you work, ask yourself what the anticipated results should be and then verify. When you become skilled at anticipating output correctly, you are surprised less often.)

If this were a real bank's data system, the files would be much larger and the data more sophisticated. However, the same design principles apply regardless of the database size. A small file gives you the ability to check the tables and see if your results are correct. Even though the data amounts are small, you need to develop the work practices to manage large amounts of data. With only a handful of records, you can easily count the number of accounts at the Campus branch. In addition to learning HOW to accomplish a task, you should learn to anticipate the computer's response to an instruction. Ask yourself what the anticipated results should be and then verify. When you become skilled at anticipating output correctly, you are surprised less often.

Identify Cascades

Cascades permit data changes to travel from one table to another.

Cascade delete searches the database and deletes all of the related records.

Cascade update connects any primary key changes to the tables in which it is a foreign key.

Cascades are an Access feature that helps update related data across tables. In databases *cascades* permit data changes to travel from one table to another. The database designer may establish cascades to update or delete related records. The string tying related items together can also make global changes to the data. If one bank branch closed and the accounts were not transferred to a different branch, the *cascade delete* feature would search the database and delete all of the accounts and customers who banked solely at the closed branch. (This may not be an optimal business practice, but it explains how the cascade delete feature works.) If a customer with an account at one branch opens a new account at a different branch, the *cascade update* will travel through the databases and connect the new account to the customer's address in the Customers table and the new account balance in the Accounts table.

As a general rule, you do not want changes cascading through the database. An inattentive data entry clerk could, with the click of a mouse, delete hundreds of records in various tables throughout the database. However, you need the power of a cascade occasionally. Suppose your company and another firm merged. Your firm has always stored customer account numbers as a five-digit number. The other firm has always used a three-digit account number. In this case you would turn the cascade update feature on; open the Customers table; and change all of the three digit numbers to five digit ones. The new account numbers would cascade through the database to any records in any table related to the Customers table—for example, the Payments or Orders tables.

Retrieve Data Rapidly by Indexing

The **indexed property** is a list that relates the field values to the records that contain the field value.

In Hands-On Exercise 1 you created the Branch table and established the BID as the primary key. Access changed the *indexed property* to Yes (No Duplicates). Access uses indexing exactly like you would read a book on U.S. history. If you need to know who succeeded Van Buren as president, you could start on page 1 and read the book in order page by page. Alternatively, you could go to the index and discover where the information about Van Buren may be found and open directly to that page. Using the index in a book makes finding (retrieving) information quicker. Indexing a database field has the same effect; it greatly reduces retrieval time. The actual index is a list that relates the field values to the records that contain the field value. Without an index, each row in the database would need to be scanned sequentially, an inefficient search method. The increased search time would adversely affect the performance of the database. All primary keys must be indexed. Additional table fields also may be indexed.

Sharing Data with Excel

Many Access and Excel tasks overlap. Although you are learning the highly valuable skill of using Access, more people know how to use Excel than Access. Therefore, a lot of data resides within Excel spreadsheets. Often the data stored in those spreadsheets fits well into an Access database design. Therefore, you need to be able to integrate existing Excel spreadsheet data into the organization's database. Fortunately, Access provides you with wizards that facilitate data sharing with Excel. Access can both import data from Excel and export data to Excel easily.

Figures 2.12–2.18 show how to use the Get External Data – Excel Spreadsheet wizard. You launch the wizard by clicking the External Data tab. Table 2.1 lists and describes the four groups on the External Data tab.

Table 2.1 Access and Other Applications Share Data

Process	When Used
Get External Data	Used to bring data into an Access database. The data sources include Excel, Other Access files, XML, SharePoint Lists, and Text files.
Export Data	Used to send a portion of a database to other applications. You might use this to create a Mail Merge letter and envelopes in Word. You could create an Excel file for a co-worker who does not know how to use (or does not have) Access, or could share your data over the Internet via a SharePoint List.
Collect and Update	You could create an e-mail mail merge to send e-mails to your clients and then use Access to manage the clients' responses.
Offline SharePoint Lists	This process might be used when traveling, if an immediate Internet connection is not available.

Launch the wizard by clicking the Excel command in the Get External Data Group.

Figure 2.12 shows the External Data tab that contains the Import Excel command. After you specify the data storage location, you can use the imported data to create a new table in Access, to *append* new records to an existing Access table, or to create a link between the Excel file and the Access table. When linked, any changes made to the Excel file will be updated automatically in the database, too.

You *append* records to an existing table by adding new records to the end of the table.

Figure 2.12 Select the Source and Destination for the Data

Figure 2.13 shows the Get External Data – Excel Spreadsheet dialog box. This feature controls where you find the data to import. It asks you to choose among three options governing what to do with the data in Access: place it in a new table, append the data to an existing table, or link the Access table to the Excel source.

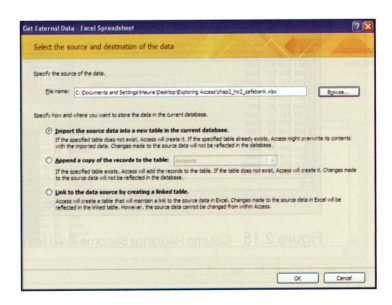

Figure 2.13 Select the Source and Destination of the Data

Figure 2.19 The Show/Hide Group and Show Table Dialog Box

Because the first time you will use the Relationship window you will be working in a newly created database, you must first use the Show Table dialog box to add the necessary tables to the Relationship window (see Figure 2.19). Select the tables you want to use in relation to other tables and add them to the Relationship window by clicking Add.

TIP Navigation Between the Relationship Window and a Table's Design

When you right-click the table title bar in the Relationship window, the shortcut menu offers you a chance to open the table in Design view. Because relationships may be established only between data with the same definition, you have a chance to check how the data in different tables have been defined.

When possible, expand the table windows to display the complete list of field names shown in the table (see Figure 2.20). You may rearrange the tables by clicking and dragging the table window title bar.

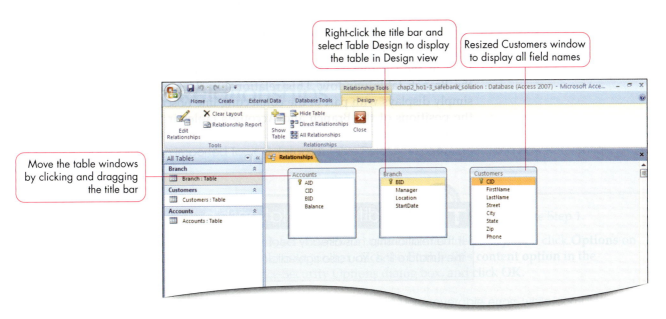

Right-click the title bar and select Table Design to display the table in Design view

Resized Customers window to display all field names

Move the table windows by clicking and dragging the title bar

Figure 2.20 The Relationship Window with Resized Tables

Establish the relationships by clicking and dragging the field name from one table to the field name in the related table. When you release the mouse, the Edit Relationships dialog box opens (see Figure 2.21). Prior to establishing a relationship, Access runs through the table data to ensure that the rules you attempt to establish in the relationship can be met. For example, it checks to make sure that the branch identification number in the Accounts table (foreign key) exactly matches a Branch ID in the Branch table where it is the primary key. If all of the Branch IDs do not match exactly between the tables, Access cannot establish the relationship with referential integrity enforced. It will attempt to make a connection, but it will warn you that a problem exists with the data.

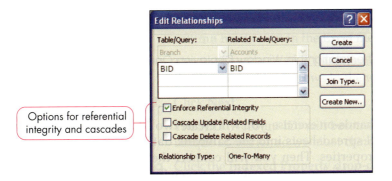

Options for referential integrity and cascades

Figure 2.21 The Edit Relationships Dialog Box

Multiple Table Database | **Access 2007** | **157**

Queries

What if you wanted to see just the customers who bank at a specific branch or who have accounts with balances over $5,000? Perhaps you need to know the customers who have accounts at multiple branches. Maybe you will need a list of all the customers who bank with the branch managed by a specific manager. The manager's name is stored in the Branch table and the customer's name in the Customers table. In this small database, you could open both tables and mentally trace through the strings of the relationships and extract the information. But in a real world database with thousands of records, you would be unable to do this accurately. A query provides the ability to ask questions based on the data or a smaller grouping of data, and to find the answers to those questions.

A *query* permits you to see the data you want arranged in the sequence that you need. It enables you to select specific records from a table (or from several tables) and show some or all of the fields for the selected records. You can perform calculations to display data that are not explicitly stored in the underlying table(s), such as the amount of interest each bank account earned during the previous month.

In this section you use the Query Wizard to create a query. You set specific conditions to display only records that meet the condition. Finally, you learn about large databases.

A *query* enables you to ask questions about the data stored in a database and returns the answers from the records in the order that matches your instructions.

Creating a Query

Create a query either by using the *Query Wizard* or specifying the tables and fields directly in Design view. Like all of the Microsoft wizards, the Query Wizard is a method to automate your work. It facilitates new query development. The results of the query display in a *dataset*, which contains the records that satisfy the criteria specified in the query.

A dataset looks and acts like a table, but it is not a table; it is a dynamic subset of a table that selects, sorts, and calculates records as specified in the query. A dataset is similar to a table in appearance and, like a table, it enables you to enter a new record or modify or delete an existing record. Any changes made in the dataset are reflected automatically in the underlying table.

The *Query Wizard* is an Access tool that facilitates new query development.

A *dataset*, which contains the records that satisfy the criteria specified in the query, provides the answers to the user's questions.

> ## TIP Changes Made to Query Results Overwrite Table Data
>
> The connection between a query result and the underlying table data may create problems. On the one hand it is to your advantage that you can correct an error in data if you should happen to spot it in a query result. You save time by not having to close the query, open the table, find the record in error, fix it, and run the query again to get robust results. On the other hand, you must be careful not to accidentally click into a query record and type something. If you press Enter or Tab, whatever you accidentally typed is stored forever in the underlying table.

The *query design grid* displays when you select a query's Design view; it divides the window into two parts.

Return to the earlier question. How would you identify the names of all of the customers who have an account at the Campus branch? Figure 2.29 contains the *query design grid* used to select customers who have accounts at the Campus Branch and further, to list those customers and their account balances alphabetically. (The design grid is explained in the next section.) Figure 2.30 displays the answer to the query in the form of a dataset.

The Customers table contains 21 records. The dataset in Figure 2.30 has only six records, corresponding to the customers who have Campus branch accounts. The records in the table are ordered by the Customer ID (the primary key), whereas the records in the dataset are in alphabetical order by last name. Changing the order of data displayed in a query has no effect on the underlying table data.

TIP | Examine the Record Number

An experienced Access user always examines the number of records returned in a query's results. As you add additional criteria, the number of records returned should decrease.

Create a Select Query

A **select query** searches the underlying tables to retrieve the data that satisfy the query parameters.

The query in Figures 2.29 and 2.30 is an example of a select query, which is the most common type of query. A **select query** searches the underlying tables to retrieve the data that satisfy the query parameters. The data display in a dataset (see Figure 2.30), which can be modified to update the data in the underlying table(s). The specifications for selecting records and determining which fields will be displayed for the selected records, as well as the sequence of the selected records, are established within the design grid of Figure 2.29. The select query is one of many different query operations Access supports.

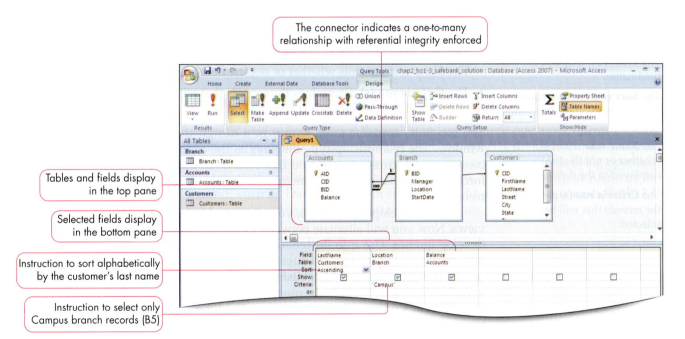

Figure 2.29 The Query Design View

moment you specify criteria in multiple fields, Access combines the fields using the And or the Or operator. When the expressions are in the same row of the query design grid, Access uses the **And operator**. This means that only the records that meet *all* criteria in all of the fields will be returned. If the criteria are positioned in different rows of the design grid, Access uses the **Or operator** and will return records meeting *any* of the specified criteria. The **Not operator** returns the *opposite* of the specification.

Figure 2.31 shows a query in Design view that specifies an And operator. It will return all of the Campus branch accounts with balances over $5,000. Both conditions must be met for the record to be included. Figure 2.32 shows a query in Design view that specifies an Or operator. It will return all of the Campus branch accounts with any balance plus all accounts at any branch with balances over $5,000. Either condition may be met for a record to be included. Figure 2.33 shows a query in Design view that specifies a Not operator. It will return all of the accounts at all of the branches excluding the Campus branch. You may combine And, Or, and Not operators to achieve the desired result. If you need a list of the accounts with balances over $5,000 at the Campus and Uptown branches, you set the criteria so that the >5000 expression is duplicated for each location specified (see Figure 2.34).

Field:	LastName	Location	Balance
Table:	Customer	Branch	Account
Sort:	Ascending		
Show:	✓	✓	✓
Criteria:		"Campus"	>5000
or:			

Figure 2.31 And Criterion—Only Records Satisfying Both Conditions Will Return

Field:	LastName	Location	Balance
Table:	Customer	Branch	Account
Sort:	Ascending		
Show:	✓	✓	✓
Criteria:		"Campus"	
or:			>5000

Figure 2.32 Or Criterion—Records Meeting Either Condition Will Return

Field:	LastName	Location	Balance
Table:	Customer	Branch	Account
Sort:	Ascending		
Show:	✓	✓	✓
Criteria:		Not "Campus"	
or:			>5000

Figure 2.33 Not Criterion—Any Record Except the Matching Will Return

Field:	LastName	Location	Balance
Table:	Customer	Branch	Account
Sort:	Ascending		
Show:	✓	✓	✓
Criteria:		"Campus"	>5000
or:		"Uptown"	>5000

Figure 2.34 And and Or Criteria—Records Meeting Both Conditions at Both Branches Return

Copying and Running a Query

After you create a query, you may want to duplicate it to use as the basis for creating similar queries. Duplicating a query saves time in selecting tables and fields for queries that need the same structure but different criteria. After you create and save one or more queries, you can execute them whenever you need them to produce up-to-date results.

Copy a Query

Sometimes you have one-of-a-kind questions about your data. Then you create and run the query, find the answer and close it. If you create the query with the wizard, you save and name it in the last step. If you create the query in Design view, it is possible for you to exit the query without saving changes. Most queries answer recurrent questions. What were sales last week in Houston, in Dallas, in Chicago? In cases like this, you set up the query for the dates and places of interest one time, then copy it, rename the copy and establish the parameters for a different city or date.

Frequently you will need to examine multiple subsets of the data. In Hands-On Exercise 3 you will create a query displaying the names and account balances of the customers who have accounts at the Campus branch. Should you need to know the same information about the customers who have Uptown accounts, you would select the query in the Navigation pane, and then copy and paste it to a blank space at the bottom pane. Right-click the copy and rename it Uptown. Open the newly created Uptown query in Design view and replace the Campus criterion with Uptown. When you run and save the query, the resulting dataset displays customers and account balances from the Uptown branch. Using this method takes you a few minutes to create branch specific queries for all five locations.

Run a Query

When you **run a query**, Access processes the query instructions and displays records that meet the conditions.

After you create the query by specifying criteria and save it, you are ready to run it. You **run a query** by clicking the Run command (the red exclamation point) to direct Access to process the instructions specified by the query. In our databases the queries run quickly. Even in the largest database you will use in the end of chapter exercises, no query will take more than a few seconds to run. As you learn how to work with these databases, keep in mind that real-world databases can be massive. Think through the query design carefully. Include all necessary fields and tables, but do not include fields or tables that are not necessary to answer the question. Unnecessary fields slow the query's run time.

Using the Query Wizard

You may create a query directly in Design view or by using the Query Wizard. Even if you initiate the query with a wizard, you will need to learn how to modify it in Design view. Often it is much faster to copy an existing query and make slight modifications to its design than it would be to start at the beginning of the wizard. You also will need to know how to add additional tables and fields to an existing query in case you failed to think through the design thoroughly and you omitted a necessary field. To launch the Query Wizard, click the Create tab and click Query Wizard in the Other group (see Figure 2.35).

Figure 2.35 Launching the Query Wizard

Access produces many different kinds of queries. Here we will work with the most common query type, the select query. This is a powerful and sophisticated tool. Select the Simple Query Wizard in the first dialog box of the Query Wizard as shown in Figure 2.36.

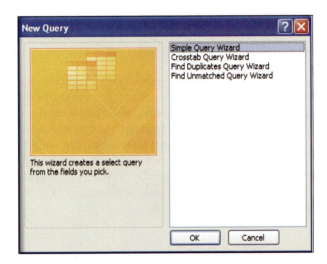

Figure 2.36 The Simple Query Wizard Step 1

In the second step of the Simple Query Wizard dialog box you specify the tables and fields needed in your query. As soon as you click on the table in the Tables/Queries drop-down box, a list of that table's fields display in the Available fields box. See Figures 2.37 and 2.38.

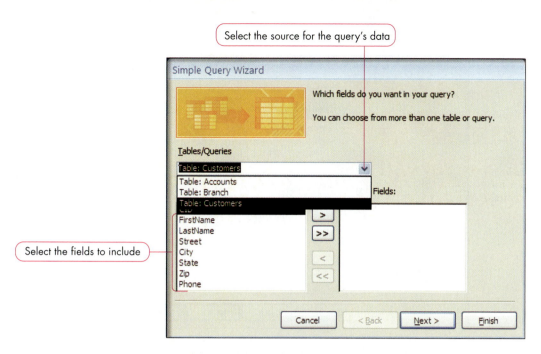

Figure 2.37 Specify which Tables or Queries to Use as Input

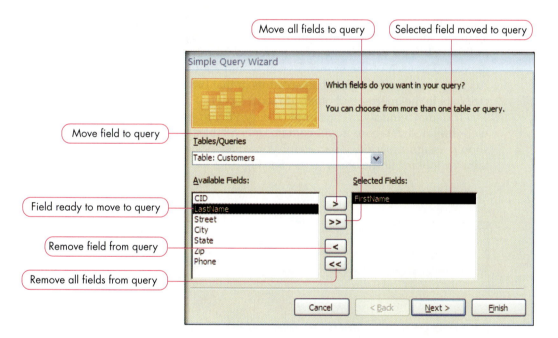

Figure 2.38 Specify the Fields for the Query

Select the necessary fields by clicking them to highlight and then using the navigation arrows described in Figure 2.39.

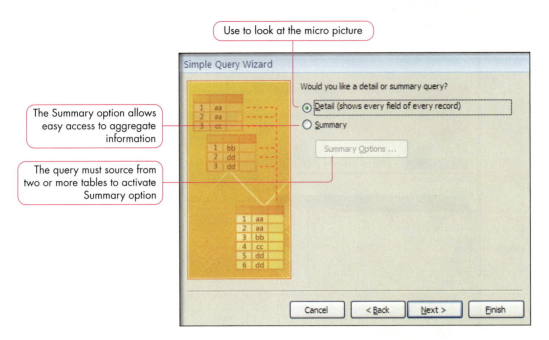

Use to look at the micro picture

The Summary option allows easy access to aggregate information

The query must source from two or more tables to activate Summary option

Figure 2.39 Select to Display Detail or to Summarize the Data

Aggregate means the collection of individual items into a total.

In the Simple Query Wizard, you choose between a detailed or a summary query. The detail query provides every record of every field. The summary enables you to aggregate data and View only summary statistics. *Aggregate* means the collection of individual items into a total. If you were only interested in the total of the funds deposited at each of the branches, you would set the query to a summary and ask Access to sum the balances of all accounts in that branch. Some Access users summarize data in the queries and others do so in reports. Either approach is acceptable.

The final window in the Simple Query Wizard directs you to name the query. A well-designed database might contain only 5 tables and 500 queries. Therefore, you should assign descriptive names for your queries so that you know what each contains by looking at the query name. See Figure 2.40.

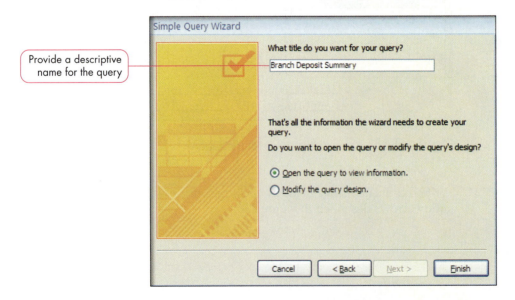

Provide a descriptive name for the query

Figure 2.40 Name the Query Descriptively

Understanding Large Database Differences

Suppose you work for a large university. You need to identify all of the students at your university who are business majors, their advisor's names, and their specific majors. The Student table contains student names, identification numbers, majors, faculty advisor's identification number, class standing, addresses, and so on. The Faculty table contains faculty names, departmental affiliation, identification number, and rank. Your query needs to include fields for the student's name, major, and the advisor's name. You would not need the student's address or the faculty member's ID because those fields are unnecessary to answer the question. You need to establish criteria to select business majors: Accounting, Finance, Information Systems, Management, Marketing, and Economics.

Even if your computer is state-of-the-art, fast, powerful, and loaded with memory, this query might take up to 15 minutes to run. If you include unnecessary fields or tables, the run time increases. At the author's university, each additional table roughly doubles the query run time. As an Access beginner, your queries might contain too much or too little information. You will make frequent modifications to the query design as you learn. As you apply your database skills to work with large databases, you will learn to carefully design queries prior to running them to minimize the time to run the queries.

In addition to the earlier mentioned size difference between real world databases and those you will use in the class, real world databases involve multiple users. Typically the organization stores the database file on the network. Multiple people may simultaneously log into the database. Each user makes changes to tables or forms. At your school, thousands of users can extract data from the university's database. Prior to meeting your advisor, you check your transcript online. You enter a database to find out how many hours you have completed and whether or not you have met the prerequisites. You have permission to view your transcript but you do not have the necessary permission to change what is recorded there. Several hundred other users have more extensive privileges in your school's database. Your Access professor can enter and probably change your grade in this class. If the securities are appropriately set on the database, your Access professor is not able to change the grade that you earned in other courses.

Most large organizations employ database administrators and managers that ensure data security, efficacy, and integrity. These professionals are well paid to make sure that no one inside or outside the firm has access to classified data or can corrupt the data resident in the system. Additionally, SOX rules mandate backup and security measures.

These positions involve a great deal of responsibility. How does someone charged with this vital role do it? One common method involves splitting the database into front and back ends. Typically the *front end* of a database contains the objects, like queries, reports, and forms, needed to interact with data, but not the tables where the record values reside. The tables are safely stored in the *back end* system where users cannot inadvertently destroy or corrupt data. Most often the front and back ends of the database are stored on different systems placed in different locations to provide an extra security measure. Users within the organization are divided into groups by their data needs. Then the groups are assigned rights and privileges. For example, a professor has privileges to record grades for students registered in his or her classes but not for other professors' classes. The financial aid officer may look at student grades and financial records, but may not alter either. The dean may look at student grades, but probably not their financial records. The student health center physician may view a student's immunization records and update it when necessary, but cannot see the student's grades.

The next hands-on exercise introduces queries as a more useful way to examine data. You use the Query Wizard to create a basic query, and then modify that query by adding an additional field and an additional table, and performing simple query criteria specifications.

The *front end* of a database contains the objects, like queries, reports, and forms, needed to interact with data, but not the tables where the record values reside.

The *back end* of the system protects and stores data so that users cannot inadvertently destroy or corrupt the organization's vital data.

CASE STUDY

Replacements, Ltd.

(Replacements, Ltd exists. The data in the case file are actual data. The customer and employee information have been changed to ensure privacy. However, the inventory and sales records reflect actual transactions.)

Today is the first day in your new position as associate marketing manager at Replacements, Ltd. In preparation for your first day on the job you have spent hours browsing the Replacements Web site, www.replacements.com. There you learned that Replacements, Ltd. (located in Greensboro, N.C.) has the world's largest selection of old and new dinnerware, including china, stoneware, crystal, glassware, silver, stainless, and collectibles. Its 300,000-square-foot facilities (the size of five football fields!) house an incredible inventory of 10 million pieces in 200,000 patterns, some more than 100 years old. While interviewing for the position, you toured the show room and warehouses. You learned that Replacements provides its customers with pieces that exactly match their

Case Study

existing patterns of china, silver, crystal, etc. People who break a cup or accidentally drop a spoon in the disposal purchase replacement treasures.

You have been given responsibility for managing several different patterns of merchandise. You need to maintain adequate inventory levels. On the one hand you need to have merchandise available so that when a customer wishes to purchase a fork in a specific pattern, the customer service representatives can find it and box it for shipment. To accomplish this task, you need to closely monitor past sales in the various patterns in order to understand purchasing habits and product demand. On the other hand, the firm cannot afford to stock inventory of patterns no one wishes to purchase. You exchange information with the customer service representatives and monitor their performance. If you discover that one of the patterns you manage has excess inventory, you will need to direct the buyers to stop purchasing additional pieces in that pattern and encourage the customer service representatives to suggest the pattern to customers. You will determine if and when a pattern should be discounted or if an incentive program or contest should be implemented to reward the sales associates for successfully selling the overstocked merchandise.

Your Assignment

- Copy the *chap3_case_replacement.accdb* file to your production folder. Name the copy **chap3_case_replacement_solution.accdb**.
- Open the Relationships window and acquaint yourself with the tables, fields, and relationships among the tables in the database.
- You need to convert the data into useful information. To accomplish this task, you will need to create a query that identifies the revenue generated from sales in each of the patterns you manage.
- You also must determine which patterns customers purchase most often.
- Replacements encourages the customer service representatives by paying them bonuses based on the orders that they fill. You will calculate each customer service representative's total sales and calculate their bonuses. The bonus will be calculated based on ½% of the representative's total sales.
- Finally, you need to compare the inventory levels of each pattern piece with its sales volume. Careful monitoring of stock levels will prevent excessive inventory. For each item calculate the percent of the inventory level that was sold in the past month. For example, if there were 100 cups in a specific pattern in inventory at the beginning of the month and 18 of them were sold during the month, the sales-inventory ratio would be 18%. Set criteria so that the zero OnHandQuantity items are excluded from the calculation.

Data Summary and Analysis

Practicing good database design discourages storing calculations as table data. Although storing calculated results in a table is not a good idea, Access *can* perform arithmetic calculations using formulae and functions much like Excel. However, the calculated results do not belong in tables. Instead, calculations needed to summarize and analyze data are found in three places: queries, forms, and reports. Professionals who use Access to develop applications within organizations have very different opinions about the most appropriate placement of calculations in Access. One group assembles and manipulates data inside a query. After you establish the calculations and criteria, the data are sent to an Access report to be cosmetically enhanced. (This is the practice that you will employ throughout the exercises in this book.) The other group does all of the calculations inside of forms and reports. This group uses fewer queries but creates far more sophisticated reports and forms.

In this section, you learn about the order of precedence and create a calculated field in a query.

Understanding the Order of Precedence

The *order of precedence* establishes the sequence by which values are calculated.

The *order of precedence* establishes the sequence by which values are calculated in an expression. Evaluate parenthetically expressed values, then exponents, multiplication and division, and, finally, addition and subtraction. Access calculates exactly what you tell it to calculate—even if your formulae are incorrect! Table 3.1 shows some examples of arithmetic order. You must have a solid understanding of these rules in order to "teach" the computer to generate the required output. Access, like Excel, uses the following symbols:

- Addition   +
- Subtraction   –
- Multiplication   *
- Division   /
- Exponentiation   ^

Creating a Calculated Field in a Query

You instruct Access to perform calculations in the Design view of the query. Create the calculated values in the first row of a blank column. You may scroll, if necessary, to find a blank column in the design grid or insert a blank column where you want

Table 3.1 Examples of Order of Precedence

Expression	Order to Perform Calculations	Output
= 2 + 3 * 3	Multiply first, and then add.	11
= (2 + 3) * 3	Add the values inside the parenthesis first, and then multiply.	15
= 2 + 2 ^ 3	Simplify the exponent first. $2^3 = 2*2*2$ or 8. Then add.	10
= (2 + 2) ^3	Add the parenthetical values first (2 + 2 = 4), and then raise the result to the 3rd power. $4^3 = 4*4*4$.	64
= 10/2 + 3	Divide first, and then add.	8
= 10/(2+3)	Add first to simplify the parenthetical expression, and then divide.	2
= 10 * 2 − 3 * 2	Multiply first, and then subtract.	14

An ***expression*** is a formula used to calculate new fields from the values in existing fields.

A ***constant*** refers to a value that does not change.

Syntax is the set of rules by which the words and symbols of an expression are correctly combined.

the calculated value to appear. A formula used to calculate new fields from the values in existing fields is also known as an ***expression***. An expression consists of a number of different items to produce the answers needed. The items used in an expression may include the following:

- Identifiers (the names of fields, controls or properties)
- Operators (arithmetic instructions about what to do with the identifiers like + or –)
- Functions (as in Excel, Access has built-in functions to perform routine calculations, like SUM or Average)
- ***Constants*** and values (numbers that may be used as a part of a calculation but are unlikely to change)

You may use the expression to perform calculations, retrieve a value from a field, set query criteria, verify data created, calculate fields or controls, and set grouping levels in reports. Access not only organizes and protects a firm's valuable data but also enables you to summarize, understand, and make decisions based on the data. Your value to an organization dramatically increases when you master the skills that surround expression building in Access.

Build Expressions with Correct Syntax

Enter the expression in the first row of the column. Using simple ***syntax*** rules you instruct the software to calculate the necessary values. You can create expressions to perform calculations using either field values or constants. You must correctly spell the field names for Access to find the appropriate values. You should assign descriptive names to the calculated fields. Access ignores spaces in calculations. The general syntax follows:

CalculatedFieldName: [InputField1] operand operator [InputField2] operand

Although this is the most appropriate format, Access enters the brackets for you if it recognizes the field name. Remember that an **operator** is a symbol, such as *, that performs some operation, such as multiplication. An **operand** is the value that is being manipulated or operated on. In calculated fields in Access, the operand is either a literal value or a field name. Figure 3.1 shows a calculated field named Interest. The calculated field first calculates the monthly interest rate by dividing the 3.5% (0.035) annual rate by 12. The monthly interest rate is then multiplied by the value in the Balance field to determine the amount of interest owed.

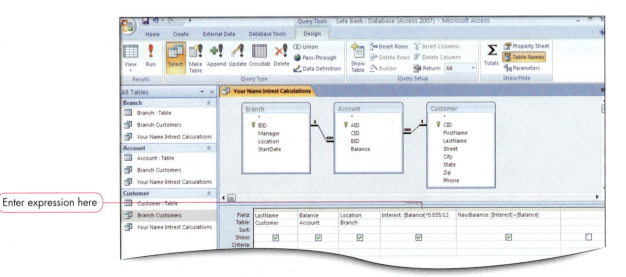

Figure 3.1 The Correct Location for a Calculated Query Expression

To help reinforce how calculated fields work, suppose you need to calculate the revenue from a purchase order. Revenue is the name of the calculated field. The following expression generates the calculated field by multiplying the unit price by the quantity ordered:

Revenue:Price*Quantity

Access enters the brackets for you and converts the expression to the following:

Revenue: [Price]*[Quantity]

For a final example of calculated fields, suppose you need to calculate a 10% price increase on all products you sell. NewPrice is the name of the calculated field. The following expression multiplies the old price by 110%:

NewPrice:Price*1.1

Access enters the brackets for you and converts the expression to the following:

NewPrice: [Price]*1.1

When you run the query, the calculated results display in the query's Datasheet view. Using the above example, Access goes to the table(s) where the prices and order quantities are stored, extracts the current data, loads it into the query, and uses the data to perform the calculation. When you direct Access to collect fields that are stored in related tables, Access uses the "strings" that form the relationship to collect the appropriate records and deliver them to the query. For example, suppose you create a query that retrieves customers' names from the customer table and the dates that the orders were placed from the Order table. The Customers table might contain 50,000 customer records. The query will return only those customers who ordered something because the relationship integrity will limit the output to only the records of interest. After the data are assembled, you can manipulate the data in each record by entering expressions. After you run the query, you need to examine the calculated results to verify that the output is what you need. Access has the ability to process a lot of numbers very quickly. Unfortunately, Access can also return incorrectly calculated results equally quickly if the formula you create is incorrect. Remember and avoid *GIGO*—Garbage In; Garbage Out!

(GIGO—Garbage In; Garbage Out!)

Verify Calculated Results

After your query runs, look at the values of the input field and then look at the calculated results returned. Ask yourself, "Does this answer make sense?" Use a pocket calculator or the Windows calculator to perform the same calculation using the same inputs and compare the answers. Alternatively, you can use Excel to check your calculated results. Copy and paste a few records into Excel. Repeat all of the calculations and compare the answers. The Access calculated field, the calculator, and the Excel calculations should return identical results.

After verifying the calculated results, you should save the query to run the next time you need to perform the same calculations.

Save a Query Containing Calculated Fields

Saving a query does *not* save the data. It saves only your instructions about what data to select and what to do with it once it is selected. Think of a query as a set of instructions directing Access to deliver data and the form the data are to assume at delivery. Writing a query is like placing an order with a restaurant server. You may order a medium rare steak, a baked potato, and tossed salad with blue cheese dressing. Your server writes the order and any special instructions and delivers it to the kitchen. In the kitchen the cook fills the order based on your instructions. Then the server delivers the ordered food to you. The data in a database is like the raw food in the kitchen. It is stored in the freezer or refrigerator or the cupboard (the tables). Data from the query (server's order) are assembled and "cooked." The big difference is that in the restaurant, once your steak is delivered to you, it is no longer available to other diners to order. The data in a database are *never* consumed. Data can be ordered simultaneously by multiple queries in a multiple user database environment. The data physically reside in the tables and never move from their storage location. Running the query collects the field values in the records of interest. The query contains only the instructions governing how Access selects and interacts with the data. If you type over a data item in a query table view, the new value automatically replaces the old one in the table.

After you run, verify, and save the query, you can use the newly created calculated fields in subsequent calculations. You may use a calculated field as input for other calculated fields. However, you must first save the query so that the calculation's results will be available.

In the first hands-on exercise you will create calculated expressions, practice verification techniques, and generate and recover from a common error.

Hands-On Exercises

1 | Calculated Query Fields

Skills covered: 1. Copy a Database and Start the Query **2.** Select the Fields, Save, and Open the Query **3.** Create a Calculated Field and Run the Query **4.** Verify the Calculated Results **5.** Recover from a Common Error

---

Step 1
Copy a Database and Start the Query

Refer to Figure 3.2 as you complete Step 1.

a. Use Windows Explorer to locate the file named *chap3_ho1-3_realestate.accdb*. Copy the file to your production folder and rename the copied file as **chap3_ho1-3_realestate_solution.accdb**.

b. Open the *chap3_ho1-3_realestate_solution.accdb* file.

c. Click **Options** on the Security Warning toolbar and then click **Enable this content** in the Microsoft Office Security Options dialog box, and click **OK**.

d. Click the **Create tab** and then click **Query Wizard** in the Other group.

e. Select **Simple Query Wizard** in the New Query dialog box. Click **OK**.

The Simple Query Wizard dialog box displays so that you can specify the table(s) and fields to include in the query design.

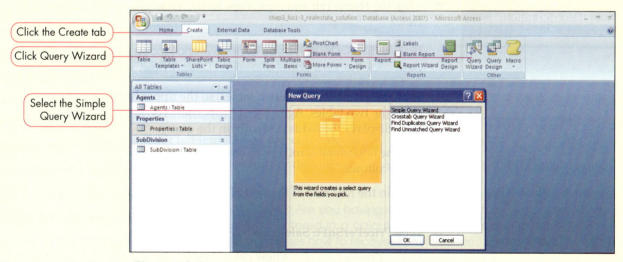

Figure 3.2 New Query Dialog Box

Step 2
Select the Fields, Save, and Open the Query

Refer to Figure 3.3 as you complete Step 2.

a. Click the **Tables/Queries drop-down arrow** and select **Table: Agents**. Double-click the **FirstName** and **LastName** fields in the **Available Fields list** to select them.

b. Click the **Tables/Queries drop-down arrow** and select **Table: Properties**. Double-click the following fields to select them: **DateListed**, **DateSold**, **ListPrice**, **SalePrice**, **SqFeet**, and **Sold**.

c. Compare your selected fields to those shown in Figure 3.3 and then click **Next**.

$10,000 earn a 3.5% interest rate, while accounts with balances below $10,000 earn only 2.75% interest. The following syntax is required for the IIf function: IIf(expr,truepart,falsepart)

IIf(Balance >= 10000, .035, .0275)

Suppose you want to calculate the number of vacation weeks an employee is eligible to receive. The firm gives two weeks of vacation to employees with five or fewer years of employment and three weeks to employees who have worked more than five years for the firm. Your query has a field showing the number of years worked, YearsWorked. The proper syntax to calculate vacation weeks is the following:

WksVacation:IIf([YearsWorked]>5, 3,2)

This expression evaluates each record and determines if the number of years worked is more than five. When the number of years is greater than 5 (true), the expression returns the number 3 in the WksVacation field, indicating that the employee receives three weeks of vacation. If the years worked are not greater than 5 (false), the expression returns 2 in the WksVacation field, indicating that the employee receives two weeks of vacation. It is important that you write the expression so that it returns only a value of True or False for every record because Access cannot deal with ambiguities. The expression always evaluates both the true and false parts for each record. When the expression, the truepart, or the falsepart references a character string (words instead of numbers), you must type the return string (the true or false parts) inside of quotation marks.

TIP   Structure IIf Logic Carefully

Even experienced Access users get surprised sometimes when using IIf functions because the false part is evaluated even when the expression is true. Occasionally this false part evaluation will result in a *divide by zero* error. You can prevent this error by rewriting the expression and reversing the inequity. For example, change > to <=. You also must reverse the truepart and falsepart actions.

When you complete the expression, click OK. The Expression Builder dialog box closes, but nothing seems to happen. You have written the instruction in a form the computer understands, but you have not yet given the command to the computer to execute your instructions. The next step is to force an execution of your command by clicking Run. Your newly calculated result displays in the Datasheet view of the table. The column heading shows the default name, Expr1. Examine and verify the results of the calculation. When you are satisfied that the results are correct, return to Design view. In the design grid, double-click <Expr1> to select it, type over <Expr1> with a descriptive field name, run, and save the query.

TIP   Calculated Field Availability

A calculated query field will not be available to use in subsequent calculations until after you save the query. When you need to make multiple-step calculations, you must author the steps one at a time, then run, verify, and save after each step.

Using the Expression Builder Steps | Reference

1. Open the query in Design view.

2. Position the insertion point in a blank column.

3. Select the Design tab.

4. Click the Builder icon to launch the Expression Builder.

5. When entering a formula, type (or click) an equal sign, =.

6. Double-click field names to add to the expression.

7. Type or click the icons for operators.

8. Double-click the Functions folder and select the type of function needed, then from the right column select the individual function.

9. Click OK to exit the Builder box.

10. Run the query.

11. Examine and verify the output.

12. Return to the Design view.

13. Highlight <Expr1> in the design grid and rename the field with a descriptive field name.

14. Run the query and save it.

Performing Date Arithmetic

> Because dates are stored as sequential numbers, you can calculate an age . . . or . . . how many days past due an invoice is.

Access, like Excel, stores all dates as serial numbers. You may format the stored dates with a format that makes sense to you. In Europe, the date *November 20, 2008*, might be formatted as *20-11-2008* or *20.11.2008*. In the United States, the same date might be formatted as *11/20/2008*, and in South Asia, the date might be formatted as *20/11/2008*. **Date formatting** affects the date's display without changing the serial value. All dates and times in Access are stored as the number of days that have elapsed since December 31, 1899. For example, January 1, 1900, is stored as 1, indicating one day after December 31, 1899. If the time were 9:00 PM on November 20, 2008, no matter how the date or time is formatted, Access stores it as 39772.857. The 39772 represents the number of days elapsed since December 31, 1899, and the .857 reflects the fraction of the 24-hour day that has passed at 9:00 PM. This storage method may seem complicated, but it affords an Access user power and flexibility when working with date values. For example, because dates are stored as sequential numbers, you can calculate the total numbers of hours worked in a week if you record the starting and ending times for each day. Using *date arithmetic* you can create expressions to calculate an age in years from a birth date, or tell a business owner how many days past due an invoice is.

Date formatting affects the date's display without changing the serial value.

Using **date arithmetic** you can create expressions to calculate lapsed time.

Identify Partial Dates with the DatePart Function

The **DatePart function** enables users to identify a specific part of a date, such as only the year.

You can look at entire dates or simply a portion of the date that is of interest. If your company increases the number of weeks of annual vacation from two weeks to three weeks after an employee has worked for five or more years, then the only part of the date of interest is the time lapsed in years. Access has a function, the **DatePart function**, to facilitate this. Table 3.3 shows the DatePart function parameters.

DatePart("yyyy",[Employees]![HireDate])

Don't let the syntax intimidate you. After you practice using the DatePart function, the syntax will get much easier to understand.

Useful date functions are:

- **Date**—Inserts the current date into an expression.
- **DatePart**—Examines a date and returns only the portion of interest.
- **DateDiff**—Measures the amount of time elapsed between two dates. This is most often today's date as determined by the date function and a date stored in a field. For example, you might calculate the number of days a payment is past due by comparing today's date with the payment DueDate.

Table 3.3 Using the DatePart Function

Function Portion	Explanation
DatePart	An Access function that examines a date and focuses on a portion of interest.
"yyyy"	The first argument, the interval, describes the portion of the date of interest. We specified the years. It could also be "dd" or "mmm".
(Employees)!(HireDate)	The second argument, the date, tells Access where to find the information. In this case, it is stored in the Employee Table in a field named HireDate.

Hands-On Exercises

2 | Expression Builder, Functions, and Date Arithmetic

Skills covered: 1. Create a Select Query **2.** Use the Expression Builder **3.** Create Calculations Using Input Stored in a Different Query or Table **4.** Edit Expressions Using the Expression Builder **5.** Use Functions **6.** Work with Date Arithmetic

---

Step 1 **Create a Select Query**	Refer to Figure 3.9 as you complete Step 1. **a.** Open the *chap3_ho1-3_realestate_solution* file if necessary, click **Options** on the Security Warning toolbar and click the **Enable this content option** in the Microsoft Office Security Options dialog box, and click **OK**.

> **TROUBLESHOOTING:** If you create unrecoverable errors while completing this hands-on exercise, you can delete the *chap3_ho1-3_realestate_solution* file, copy the *chap3_ho1_realestate_solution* backup database you created at the end of the first hands-on exercise, and open the copy of the backup database to start the second hands-on exercise again.

b. Open the **Agents table** and replace **Angela Scott's** name with your name. Close the Agents table.

c. Click the **Create tab** and click **Query Wizard** in the Other group. Select **Simple Query Wizard** and click **OK**.

d. Select the fields (in this order) from the Agents table: **LastName** and **FirstName**. From the Properties table select **DateListed, DateSold, ListPrice, SalePrice**, and **SqFeet**. From the SubDivision table select the **Subdivision** field. Click **Next**.

You have selected fields from three related tables. Because relationships exist among the tables, you can trust that the agent's name that returns when the query runs will be the agent associated with the property.

e. Check to make sure that the option for a detail query is selected and click **Next**.

f. Name this query **YourName Commissions** and click **Finish**.

The query should run and open in Datasheet view. An experienced Access user always checks the number of records when a query finishes running and opens. This query should have 54 records. See Figure 3.9.

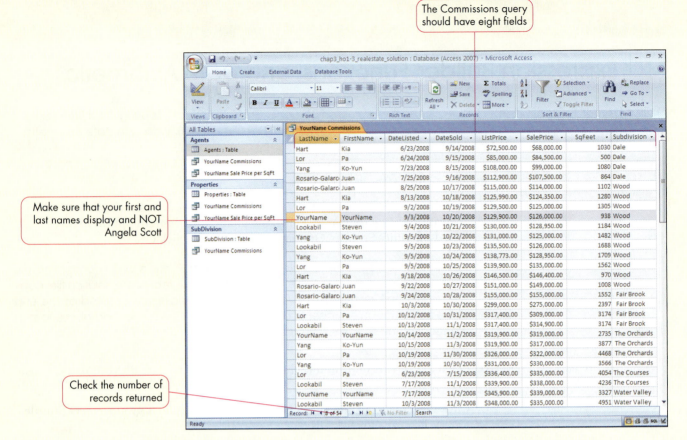

The Commissions query should have eight fields

Make sure that your first and last names display and NOT Angela Scott

Check the number of records returned

Figure 3.9 Datasheet View of the YourName Commissions Query

Step 2
Use the Expression Builder

Refer to Figure 3.10 as you complete Step 2.

a. Click the **Home tab** and switch to Design view. Scroll to the right to locate the first empty column in the design grid and position your insertion point in the first row.

b. Verify that the Design tab is selected and click **Builder** in the Query Setup group.

The Expression Builder dialog box opens. You may click the title bar and reposition it to a more convenient location if necessary.

c. Repeat the PricePerSqFt calculation from Hands-On Exercise 1 by using the Expression Builder. Click or type =.

d. Locate the list of fields in the Commissions query in the middle column and double-click the **SalePrice** field.

The work area of the Expression Builder dialog box should now display = [SalePrice]. The Expression Builder adds the **brackets** and always spells the field names correctly.

e. Click or type the divide operator (the forward slash, /) and then double-click the **SqFeet** field name in the middle column.

Now the work area of the expression builder will display = [SalePrice] / [SqFeet].

f. Click **OK**. Run the query. Scroll right in the Datasheet view to find the newly calculated field, which is named Expr1.

g. Verify the results of the calculation.

The fifth record has values that can be rounded more easily in your head—$114,000 and 1102 Sq. Ft. That should return a result slightly higher than $100. The actual result is 0103.44. Once you are satisfied with the accuracy of the calculation, continue with the next step.

h. Activate the **Home tab** (if necessary) and change the view to Design view.

TIP   Switching Between Design and Datasheet Views

An easy way to alternate views for an Access object is to right-click the object window's title bar and select the appropriate view from the shortcut menu. You can also click the views buttons in the bottom-right corner of the Access window. In this case, the object title bar says YourName Commissions. See Figure 3.10 for instructions on where to right-click.

i. Double-click **Expr1** in the field row of the right column. Type **PricePerSqFt**.

j. Right-click the field text box in the design grid that contains the PricePerSqFt calculated field. Select **Properties** from the shortcut menu. Click the **Format drop-down arrow** in the Property Sheet window and select **Currency**. Click the X to close the Property Sheet window.

k. Run the query. Click **Save** (or press **Ctrl + S**) and return to Design view.

l. Click the insertion point in the Field row of the first empty column and activate the Expression Builder. Look in the middle column that shows the list of available fields in this query. The last listed field should be the newly saved PricePerSqFt.

TROUBLESHOOTING: Sometimes you need to edit an expression created using the Expression Builder. When you open the Expression Builder to make the edits, you will find that Access adds <Expr1> to any unsaved expressions. Locate and double-click the <Expr1> to select it and delete it prior to making the necessary edits to the expression.

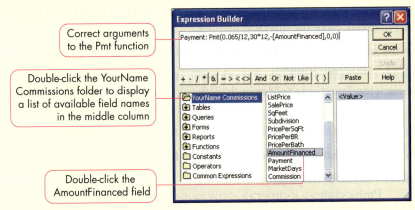

Correct arguments to the Pmt function

Double-click the YourName Commissions folder to display a list of available field names in the middle column

Double-click the AmountFinanced field

Figure 3.13 The Payment Function Arguments

Step 6
Work with Date Arithmetic

Refer to Figure 3.14 as you complete Step 6.

a. Position the insertion point in the field row of the first blank column of the query in Design view. Launch the Expression Builder.

You are going to calculate the number of days that each property was on the market prior to its sale.

b. Enter the formula **= [DateSold] – [DateListed]**. Run the query. Return to Design view and replace Expr1 with **MarketDays**. Save the query. Open the Property Sheet window and *format* the field as **Fixed** and set the *Decimal Places* to **0**.

Because Access stores all dates as serial numbers, the query returns the number of days on the market. The first property was placed on the market on June 23, and it sold on September 14. Look at your query result. This property was for sale all of July, all of August, and for parts of June and September. This is about three months. Does the query result reflect about three months?

c. Create a new field. Use the Expression Builder to multiply the SalePrice field by the commission rate of 7%. The formula in the Expression Builder is **= [SalePrice] * .07**. Run the query and replace Expr1 with **Commission**. Save the query.

The Commission calculated field calculates the total commission. The agent earns 7% of the sale price. The first agent's commission is 4760.

d. Right-click the Commission calculated field. Select **Properties** from the shortcut menu. Click the **Format drop-down arrow** in the Property Sheet window and select **Currency**. Click the **X** to close the Property Sheet window.

The values in the Commission calculated field now appear in Currency format. The first agent's commission displays as $4,760.00.

e. Click the **Office Button**, select **Manage**, and then select **Back Up Database**. Enter the filename **chap3_ho2_realestate_solution** (note *ho2* instead of *ho1-3*) and click **Save** on the Quick Access Toolbar.

You just created a backup of the database after completing the second hands-on exercise. The original database *chap3_ho1-3_realestate_solution* remains onscreen. If you ruin the original database as you complete the third hands-on exercise, you can use the backup file you just created.

f. Close the file and exit Access if you do not want to continue with the next exercise at this time.

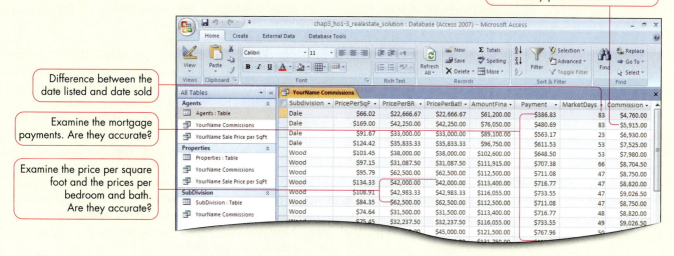

This property sold for $84,500. The commission rate is 7%. Does $5,915 reflect 7% of the sale price? Did you use a calculator or Excel to verify your calculation?

Difference between the date listed and date sold

Examine the mortgage payments. Are they accurate?

Examine the price per square foot and the prices per bedroom and bath. Are they accurate?

Figure 3.14 Verify, Verify, Verify!

Data Aggregates

Assume that you have an old-fashioned bank that still sends paper statements at the end of the month through the mail. Your statement arrives at your mailbox, and you open it. What is the first thing that you examine? If you are like most people, you first look at the balance for each account. The checking account information lists each transaction during the last month, whether it is a deposit or withdrawal, and the transaction method—ATM or paper check. These records provide vitally important data. But, the information contained in the account balances gives you a summarized snapshot of your financial health. You may then use the balance information to make decisions. "Yes, I can buy those concert tickets!" or "No, I better buy nothing but gas and groceries until payday." Your bank statement provides you with summary information. Your account balances are data aggregates.

> A **data aggregate** is a collection of many parts that come together from different sources and are considered a whole.

A **data aggregate** is a collection of many parts that come together from different sources and are considered a whole. Commonly employed aggregating calculations include sum, average, minimum, maximum, standard deviation, and variance. Access provides you with many methods of summarizing or aggregating data. Decision makers use the methods to help make sense of an array of choices.

In this section, you learn how to create and work with data aggregates. Specifically, you learn how to use the totals row and create a totals query.

Creating and Working with Data Aggregates

> A **total row** displays as the last row in the Datasheet view of a table or query and provides a variety of summary statistics.

Aggregates may be used in a query, table, form, or report. Access provides two methods of adding aggregate functions to a query. A **total row** displays as the last row in the Datasheet view of a table or query and provides a variety of summary statistics. The first method enables you to add a total row from the Datasheet view. This method is quick and easy, works in the Datasheet view of a table, and has the additional advantage that it provides the total information without altering the object design. You will recall that some databases are split into front and back end portions. Different users have different levels of privileges when interacting with the database. Adding a total row to a query or table can be accomplished by the lowest-privilege-level employee because it does not alter the structure of the object. The second method enables you to alter the query design and create a totals query. This method has the advantage of permitting you to group your data into relevant subcategories. For example, you can subtotal all houses sold in a specific subdivision or by each salesperson. After the summary statistics are assembled, you can employ them to make decisions. Who is the leading salesperson? In which neighborhood do houses sell most often or least often? This method requires that the user have rights to alter the design of a query. In a large, split database, a front-end user may not be afforded the rights to create or alter a query design. The query design is generally restricted to back-end users—the IT professionals only.

Data aggregation gives the decision maker a powerful and important tool. The ability to summarize and consolidate mountains of data into a distilled and digestible format makes the Access software a popular choice for managerial users. You already have learned that data aggregates may be created in queries. Access also permits aggregation in reports. In the first section you learned that some users calculate all of their expressions in queries, whereas others perform needed calculations in forms and reports. The positioning of data aggregates also may be accomplished in a variety of ways. Some users aggregate and calculate summary statistics in queries, others in reports. You will need to learn both methods of aggregation because the practices and procedures governing database use differ among firms. Some firms allow users relatively free access to both the front and rear ends of the database; other firms grant extremely limited front-end rights only.

Create a Total Row in a Query or Table

Figure 3.15 illustrates adding a total row to the Datasheet view. Access can total or average numeric fields only. Begin by positioning your insertion point in a numeric or currency field of any record. Then click Totals in the Records group on the Home tab. The word Total is added below the new record row of the query. The highlighted numeric field shows a box with an arrow in the Total row. You may choose from several different aggregate functions by clicking the arrow. This method works in the same way if you want to add a total row to a numeric field in a table.

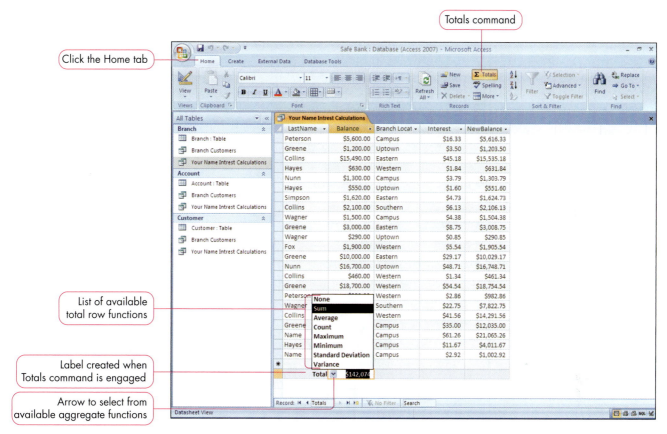

Figure 3.15 Adding a Total Row to a Query in Datasheet View

Group Totals in a Totals Query

The Total row, when added to a query, provides the decision maker with useful information. However, it does not provide any method of subtotaling the data. The total row is useful when a decision maker needs to know the totals or averages of all the data in a query or table. Sometimes knowing only the total is insufficient. The decision maker needs to know more detail. For example, knowing the total sales of houses during a period is good information. Knowing subtotals by salespeople would be more useful. Knowing subtotals by subdivision also would be useful information. Instead of using a total row, you can create a ***totals query*** to organize the results of a query into groups to perform aggregate calculations. It contains a minimum of two fields. The first field is the grouping field, such as the salesperson's last name. The second field is the numeric field that the decision maker wishes to summarize, such as the sale price of the homes. You may add other numeric fields to a totals query to provide additional information. The totals query in Access helps you provide a more detailed snapshot of the data.

The SafeBank database that you created in Chapter 2 has five branch locations. If you need to know the total deposits by location, you would create a totals query. The two fields necessary would be the Location field in the Branch table and the Account

A ***totals query*** organizes query results into groups by including a grouping field and a numeric field for aggregate calculations.

> A totals query can only include the field or fields that you want to total and the grouping field.

Balance field in the Accounts table. After you create and run the query, you may add parameters to limit the totals query to a specific data subset. The process of adding criteria in a totals query is identical to any other query. Remember that a totals query can include only the field or fields that you want to total and the grouping field. No additional descriptive fields are allowed in the totals query. If you need to see the salesperson's last name, the sale price of the house, *and* the salesperson's first name, you would need to create two queries. The first query would be the totals query summarizing the sales data by last name. Then you would need to create a second query based on the totals query and add the additional descriptive field (the first name) to the new query. Figure 3.16 shows the setup for a totals query.

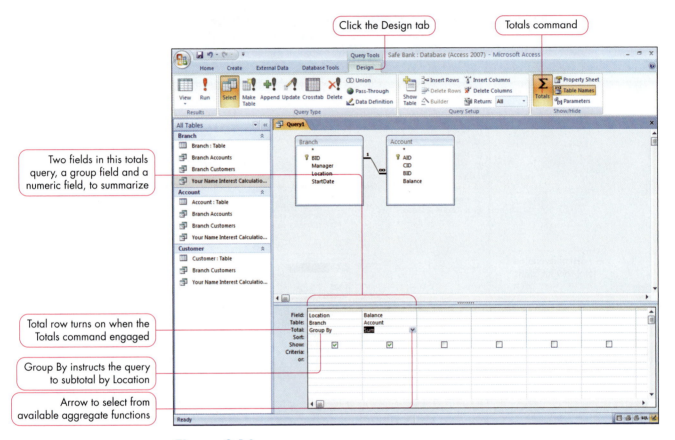

Figure 3.16 Constructing a Totals Query

Hands-On Exercises

3 | Data Aggregates

Skills covered: 1. Add a Total Row **2.** Create a Totals Query Based on a Select Query **3.** Add Fields to the Design Grid **4.** Add Grouping Options and Specify Summary Statistics

---

Step 1	Refer to Figure 3.17 as you complete Step 1.
Add a Total Row	

Refer to Figure 3.17 as you complete Step 1.

a. Open the *chap3_ho1-3_realestate_solution* file if necessary, click **Options** on the Security Warning toolbar and click the **Enable this content option** in the Microsoft Office Security Options dialog box, and click **OK**.

> **TROUBLESHOOTING:** If you create unrecoverable errors while completing this hands-on exercise, you can delete the *chap3_ho1-3_realestate_solution* file, copy the *chap3_ho2_realestate_solution* backup database you created at the end of the first hands-on exercise, and open the copy of the backup database to start the second hands-on exercise again.

b. Open the **YourName Commissions query** in the Datasheet view.

c. Click the **Home tab** and click **Totals** in the Records group.

Look at the last row of the query. The Totals command is a toggle: Click it once to display the Total row. Click it again to hide the Total row. You need the Total row turned on to work the next steps.

d. Click in the cell that intersects the **Total row** and the **SalePrice** column.

This is another place in Access that when selected, a drop-down list becomes available. Nothing indicates that the drop-down menu exists until the cell or control is active. You need to remember that this is one of those places in order to aggregate the data.

e. Click the **drop-down arrow** and select **Sum** to calculate the total of all the properties sold. Widen the SalePrice field if you can't see the entire total value.

The total value of the properties sold is $19,936,549.00.

f. Scroll right, locate the **Subdivision field,** and click in the Total row to activate the drop-down list.

The choices from the total list are different. You may have the summary statistics set to None or Count. Subdivision is a character field. Access recognizes that it cannot add or average words and automatically limits your options to only tasks that Access is able to do with words.

g. Select **Count** from the drop-down list in the Total row for the Subdivision field.

h. Click in the **Total row** in the **PricePerSqFt** field. Click the **drop-down arrow** and select **Average**.

i. Click in any record of any field. Close the query.

A dialog box opens that asks if you wish to save the changes to the *layout* of the YourName Commissions query. It does NOT ask if you wish to save the changes made to the design. Toggling a Total row on and off is a layout (cosmetic) change only and does not affect the architectural structure of the query or table design.

j. Click **Yes**. The query saves the layout changes and closes.

h. Return to Design view. Position the insertion point in the first blank column in the Field row. Click **Builder** in the Query Setup group on the Design tab. In the **left column**, open the folder for **functions**. Open the **Built-In Functions** folder. Scroll the **right column** to locate the **IIf** function. Double-click to insert the function.

i. Double-click **<<expr>>** and replace it with **[Performance] = "Excellent"**; double-click **<<truepart>>** and replace it with **1000**; double-click **<<falsepart>>** and replace it with **0**. (That is zero, not the letter O.)

j. Run the query. Return to the Design view and double-click **Expr1** in the field row of the last column. Type **Bonus**. Run and save the query. Close the database.

2 Comfort Insurance—Vacation

The Comfort Insurance Agency is a midsized company with offices located across the country. The human resource office is located in the home office in Miami. Each year, each employee receives a performance review. The review determines employee eligibility for salary increases and the annual performance bonus. The employee data are stored in an Access database. This database is used by the human resource department to monitor and maintain employee records. Your task is to calculate the salary increase for each employee, the number of years they have worked for the firm, and the number of vacation days they are eligible to receive. You are the human resource department manager. If you correctly calculate the employee salaries and vacations, you will receive a bonus. Work carefully and check the accuracy of the calculations. This project follows the same set of skills as used in Hands-On Exercises 1 and 2 in this chapter. The instructions are less detailed to give you a chance to practice your skills. If you have problems, feel free to reread the detailed directions presented in the chapter. Compare your results to Figure 3.23.

a. Copy the partially completed file *chap3_pe2_insurance.accdb* to your production folder. Rename it **chap3_pe2_insurance_solution.accdb**, open the copied file, and enable the security content.

b. Click the **Database Tools tab** and then click **Relationships** in the Show/Hide group. Examine the table structure, relationships, and fields. Once you are familiar with the database, close the Relationships window.

c. Create a new query using the Query Wizard. Click the **Create tab** and click **Query Wizard** in the Other group. Select **Simple Query Wizard** in the first screen of the dialog box. Click **OK**.

d. Add fields to the query. From the **Employees table** select the **LastName, FirstName, HireDate**, and **Salary** fields. From the **Titles table** select the **2008Increase** field. Click **Next**. This needs to be a detail query. Name the query **Your_Name Raises and Tenure**. Click **Finish**.

e. Switch to Design view by right-clicking the query window tab and selecting **Design View** from the shortcut menu.

f. Position the insertion point in the first blank column in the Field row. Create an expression by typing **2008Raise:[Salary]*[2008Increase]**. Format it as **Currency**.

...continued on Next Page

g. Click **Run** in the Results group on the Design tab. Look at the output in the Datasheet view. Verify that your answers are correct. If they are, save the query.

h. Return to Design view. Position the insertion point in the first blank column in the Field row. Click **Builder** in the Query Setup group on the Design tab. In the left column, open the folder for functions. Open the Built-In Functions folder. Scroll the right column to locate the **DatePart** function. Double-click to insert the function to the work area.

i. Double-click <<*interval*>> in the function in the work area of the Expression Builder dialog box. Type, **"yyyy"**. Double-click <<*date*>> and replace it with **[HireDate]**. Delete the rest of the arguments and commas but do not delete the closing parenthesis. Your expression should look like this:

DatePart ("yyyy", [HireDate])

j. Run and verify the output. Return to Design view and replace Expr1 in the field row of the last column with **YearHired**. Save the query.

k. Use the Expression Builder or type to create an expression that measures how long each employee has worked. Assume that this year is 2008. The finished expression will look like this:

YearsWorked:2008 – [YearHire]

l. Run and save the query. Sort the output in descending order by the YearsWorked field. Close the database.

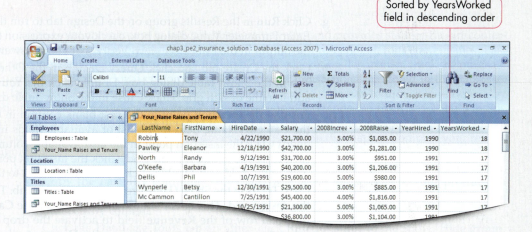

Figure 3.23 Raises and Tenure

3 Northwind Traders

Northwind Traders is a small, international, specialty food company. It sells products in eight different divisions: beverages, confections (candy), condiments, dairy products, grains and cereals, meat and poultry, produce, and seafood. The company offers discounts to some customers. Different customers receive differing discount amounts. The firm purchases merchandise from a variety of suppliers. All of the order and inventory information is stored in the company's database. This database is used by the marketing department to monitor and maintain sales records. You are the marketing manager. Your task is to determine the revenue from each order and to summarize the revenue figures by product category. This project follows the same set of skills as used in Hands-On Exercises 2 and 3 in this chapter. The instructions are less detailed to give you a chance to practice your skills. If you have problems, feel free to reread the detailed directions presented in the chapter. Compare your results to Figure 3.24.

...continued on Next Page

CASE STUDY
Northwind Traders

Northwind Traders is a small, international, specialty food company. It sells products in eight different divisions: beverages, confections (candy), condiments, dairy products, grains and cereals, meat and poultry, produce, and seafood. Although most of its customers are restaurants and gourmet food shops, it has a few retail customers, too. All of the order information is stored in the company's database. This database is used by the finance department to monitor and maintain sales records. You are the finance manager. Your task is to determine

Case Study

the revenue from each order and to summarize the first-quarter revenue for each month and by each category. You need only report on gross revenue—the total amount the firm receives. This report does not need to calculate any costs or expenses. It is important that you report accurately. Figure 4.1 presents a rough layout of the report. You must identify the source data; prepare a report; and group it to match the layout.

Your Assignment

- Copy the file named *chap4_case_traders.accdb*. Rename the copy **chap4_case_traders_solution.accdb**. Open the copied file and enable the content.
- Locate and rename the Your Name Revenue query with your first and last name. Use this query as the source for your report. It contains all the needed fields for the report plus several fields you do not need.
- Create a report based on the Your Name Revenue query. Use any report creation method you learned about in the chapter.
- Add appropriate grouping levels to produce the output shown in Figure 4.1. Name the report **Your Name First Quarter Sales by Month and Category**. You may select formatting as you want, but the grouping layout should match the design shown.
- Print the completed report.
- Compact and repair the file.
- Back up the database.

Appearances Matter

By now you know how to plan a database, create a table, establish relationships among table data, and extract, manipulate, and summarize data using queries. You generated output by printing table or query datasheets. If you look back at your earlier work, you will see that the information exists, but it is bland. You probably have worked in other application software sufficiently to wonder if Access can enhance the print files. Access provides a powerful tool, giving you the ability to organize and present selected data clearly. Most of the printed output generated by Access users comes from reports.

Enhanced data improves the functionality of database information. Just as in the other Microsoft Office applications, you can change the size, style, and placement of printed matter. You may highlight portions of output to call attention to them. You may also add graphs, pictures, or charts to help the report reader more easily convert the database data into useful information. Designing and producing clear, functional, and organized reports facilitates decision-making. Report production begins with planning the report's design.

In this section, you plan reports. First you create reports using the Report Tool, and then you edit the report by using the Layout view.

Planning a Report

A **report** is a printed document that displays information from a database.

A **report** is a printed document that displays information from a database in a manner that provides clear information to managers. You can design a report to create a catalog, a telephone directory, a financial statement, a graph showing sales by month, a shipping label, or a letter to customers reminding them about a past due payment. All documents you create using table data are Access reports. You should carefully consider what information you need and how you can optimally present it.

Access provides powerful tools to help you accomplish this goal. However, if you do not take the time to plan the report in advance, the power of the tools may impede the report process. You should think through what elements you need and how they should be arranged on the printed page prior to launching the software. The time invested planning the report's appearance at the start of the process leads to fewer surprises with the end result. The report plan helps you take charge of the computer instead of the computer controlling you.

(The report plan helps you take charge of the computer instead of the computer controlling you.)

Draw a Paper Design

The most important tool you use to create an Access report may be a pencil. If you sketch your desired output before touching the mouse, you will be happier with the results. As you sketch, you must ask a number of questions.

- What is the purpose of the report?
- Who uses this report?
- What elements, including labels and calculations, need to be included? What formulae will produce accurate results?
- Will the results be sensitive or confidential? If so, does there need to be a warning printed on the report?
- How will the report be distributed? Will users pull the information directly from Access or will they receive it through e-mail, a fax, the Internet, Word, or Excel?

Sketch the report layout on paper. Identify the field names, their locations, their placement on the page, and other design elements as you sketch. Figure 4.1 provides a sample report layout.

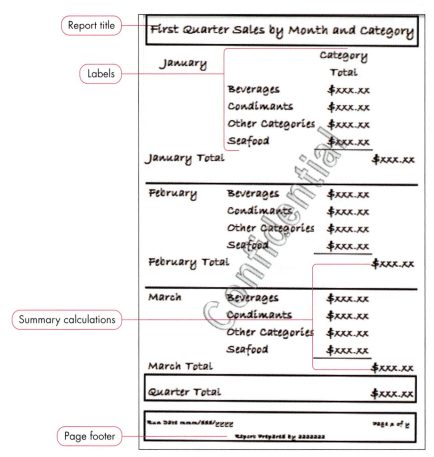

Report title
Labels
Summary calculations
Page footer

Figure 4.1 Report Plan

Identify Data Sources

In the next step of planning your report, you need to identify the data source(s) of each report element. You may use one or more tables, queries, or a combination of tables and queries as the report's source. Occasionally, a single table or query contains all of the records you need for the report. Typically, however, you need to specify several tables. When multiple tables are needed to create a report, you may assemble all necessary data in a single query and then base the report on that query. Reports frequently contain graphics as well as data. As you identify the sources of report input, you also need to specify the graphic source. Frequently, a company logo on an invoice or a watermark, indicating that the material is confidential or proprietary, is printed on the report.

Select a Reporting Tool

Access gives you several tools to facilitate report creation. Which one you select depends on the data source and complexity of the report design. Table 4.1 summarizes the available tools and their usage.

Table 4.1 Report Tools, Location, and Usage

Report Tool	Location	Data Source	Output Complexity
Report Tool	Create Tab, Reports Group, Reports command	Single table or query	Limited. This creates a report showing all of the fields in the data source.
Report Wizard	Create Tab, Reports Group, Report Wizard command	Single or multiple tables or queries or a mixture of tables and queries	More sophisticated. Include (or exclude) fields. Add grouping and sorting instructions. Choose between detailed or summary data presentation.
Label Wizard	Create Tab, Reports Group, Labels command	Single or multiple tables or queries or a mixture of tables and queries	Limited. This feature only produces mailing labels (or name badges) but does so formatted to fit a variety of commercially available mailing labels. The output displays in multiple columns only in Print Preview. Filterable to exclude records.
Blank Report	Create Tab, Reports Group, Blank Report command	Single or multiple tables or queries or a mixture of tables and queries	Limited and extremely complex. Use to quickly assemble a few fields from multiple tables without stepping through the wizard. Alternatively, use to customize the most sophisticated reports with complex grouping levels and sorts.

Using Different Report Views

You have worked with Datasheet and Design views of tables and queries to perform different tasks. For example, you cannot perform data entry in an Access table in Design view, nor can you establish query criteria in Datasheet view. Similarly, Access 2007 provides different views of your report. You view and edit the report using different views depending on what you need to accomplish. Because Access reports may be more sophisticated than queries or tables, you have more views available. Each view accommodates different actions.

Use Print Preview

The *Print Preview* displays the report as it will be printed.

The *Print Preview* displays the report exactly as it will appear on the printed output. You may look at or print your reports in this view, but you cannot edit the report data. You may specify which pages to print in the Print dialog box. The default value will print all pages in the report. Figure 4.2 shows an Access report in Print Preview.

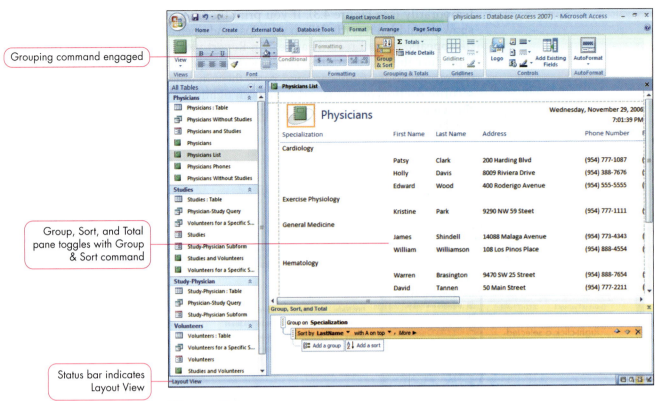

Grouping command engaged

Group, Sort, and Total pane toggles with Group & Sort command

Status bar indicates Layout View

Figure 4.4 Report in Layout View with Grouping and Sorting

Perfect a Report in Design View

The **Design view** displays the report's infrastructure but no data.

The **Design view** displays the report's infrastructure design, but it does not display data. It provides you the most powerful method of viewing an Access report. You may perform many of the same tasks in Design view as you can in Layout view—add and delete fields, add and remove sorting and grouping layers, rearrange data elements, adjust column widths, and customize report elements. You do not see any of the report's data while in this view. When the report is very lengthy, hiding the data as you alter the design may be an advantage because you save time by not scrolling. However, the Design view looks so different from the final output, it may be confusing. You need to experiment with using both the Layout and Design views and decide which view fits your style. Figure 4.5 displays the Physicians report in Design view. The next section provides explanations for all of the little boxes and stripes.

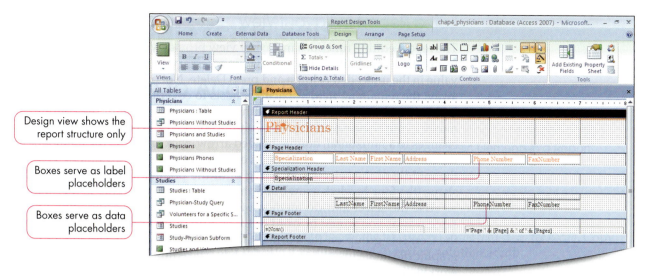

Design view shows the report structure only

Boxes serve as label placeholders

Boxes serve as data placeholders

Figure 4.5 Reports Shown in Design View Do Not Display Record Values

Create and Edit a Report

Access gives you several different methods to generate a report. You will first learn how to use the Report tool. Start by determining all of the fields needed for the report. To use the Report tool, you need to assemble all of the necessary data in one place. This tool is extremely easy to use and will adequately serve your needs much of the time. Occasionally, a table contains all of the fields for a report. More often, you will need to create or open a query containing the necessary fields. If an existing query has all of the fields needed for the report but also some unneeded fields, you will probably use the existing query. You can delete the extraneous fields.

Create a Report with the Report Tool

First you need to determine the record source for the report. Open the record source in Datasheet view. Click the Create tab and click Report in the Reports group. Access creates the report and displays it in Layout view (see Figure 4.6). If you like the look of the report, you may print, save, and close it from the Layout view. When you reopen the saved report file, Access automatically returns to the record source and loads the most recent data into the report.

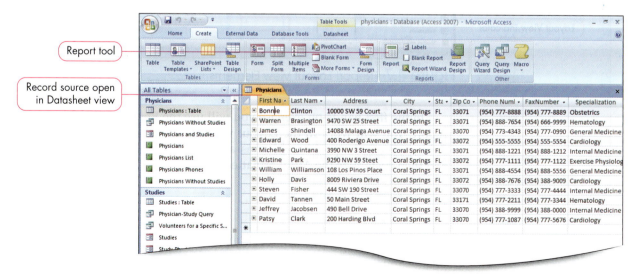

Report tool

Record source open in Datasheet view

Figure 4.6 Set Up for Using Report Tool

Refer to Figure 4.9 as you complete Step 2.

a. Right-click **Your Name** in the LastName field and select **Equals "Your Name"** from the shortcut menu.

You have created and applied a filter that displays only your orders. The status bar in the lower-right corner of the window tells you that the report has a filter applied. Only your records should display.

b. Right-click the word *Miami* and select **Does Not Equal "Miami"** from the shortcut menu.

Additional records are filtered out of the report, and a total for the Revenue field moves into view. Note that the total did not inherit the currency format from the source data. You may need to scroll right to see the total of the Revenue column.

c. Compare your selected fields to those shown in Figure 4.9 and then click **Save**.

The Save As dialog box opens with the default name (inherited from the source query) highlighted.

d. Type **Your Name Sales Outside of Miami**. Click **OK**.

e. Close the report and close the query.

You saved the report based on the query, so it no longer needs to be open. Although this is a small database, working with unnecessary objects open may slow your computer's response time. You should always close unnecessary objects.

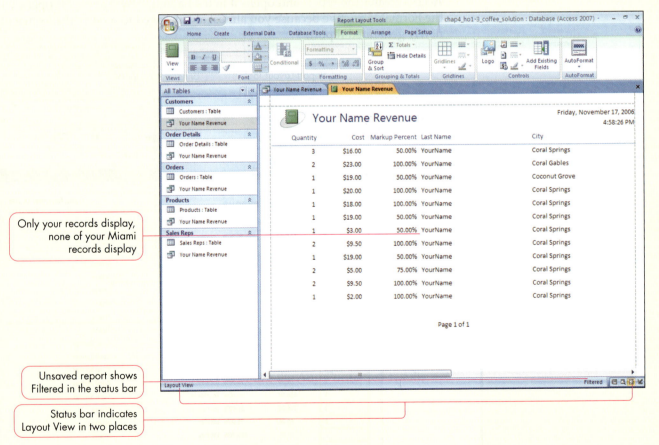

Only your records display, none of your Miami records display

Unsaved report shows Filtered in the status bar

Status bar indicates Layout View in two places

Figure 4.9 Filtered, Totaled Report

Step 3
Remove Fields from a Report and Adjust Column Widths

Refer to Figure 4.10 as you complete Step 3.

a. Open the **Your Name Sales Outside of Miami report**. Look at the right side of the status bar. It displays *Report View*. The status bar no longer indicates that the report is filtered.

When you reopen an existing report, it opens in Report view. This view lets you look at the report and permits limited filtering capabilities. Because this view provides limited editing interaction, you need to change to Layout view.

b. Right-click the **Your Name Sales Outside of Miami tab** and select **Layout View** from the shortcut menu.

c. Click the label **Quantity**.

A gold box surrounds the selected field name, and a dotted border surrounds the record values in the field.

TROUBLESHOOTING: The gold box should only be around the word Quantity. If it surrounds the entire label row, you are still in Report view. Switch to Layout view and then click Quantity again.

d. Press **Delete**.

The column disappears from the report. The remaining columns move left to fill the empty space.

e. Click **your name** in any record. Move your mouse to the right boundary of the gold border and, when the pointer shape changes to a double-headed arrow, click and drag the boundary to the left to decrease the column width.

f. Click a **city name** in any record. Move your mouse to the right boundary of the gold border and, when the pointer shape changes to a double-headed arrow, click and drag the boundary to the left to decrease the column width.

The report should fit on a single page now. You notice that the column heading for the Markup Percent column is much wider than the values in the column.

g. Click the **Markup Percent** column label to activate the gold border. Single-click **Markup Percent** again to edit the label.

You know you are in edit mode because the border color changes to black, and a flashing insertion point appears inside the border.

h. Position the insertion point to the left of the *P* in *Percent*. Press **Ctrl+Enter**. Click anywhere on the report to exit edit mode. Save the report.

The Ctrl+Enter command forces a line break. The word *Percent* moves below the word *Markup*.

TIP Forced Line Break

A similar command, Alt+Enter, may be used in Excel to force a line break, when the width of the column name greatly exceeds the width of the data displayed in the column. Although word wrapping may achieve the same effect, you can more precisely control which word prints on what line by forcing the break yourself.

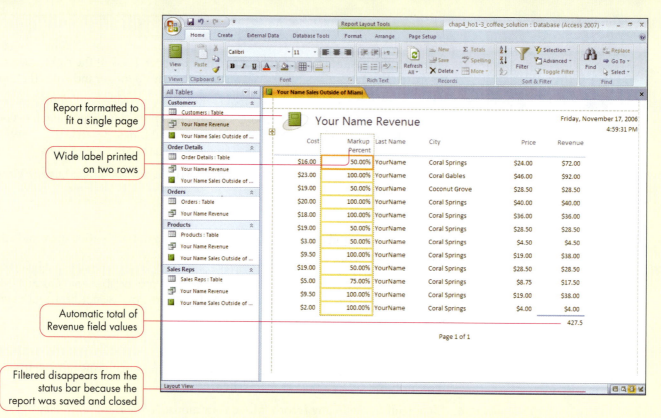

Report formatted to fit a single page

Wide label printed on two rows

Automatic total of Revenue field values

Filtered disappears from the status bar because the report was saved and closed

Figure 4.10 Resized Report

Step 4
Reposition Report Objects and Insert Graphic Elements in a Report

Refer to Figure 4.11 as you complete Step 4.

a. Click any record in the **City** column to select it. Move the mouse to the middle of the selected column. When the pointer shape changes to a *four-headed arrow*, click and drag to the left until the vertical gold line is on the left edge of the report. Release the mouse.

As you drag past other columns in the report, a gold line moves to tell you the column's current position. When you release the mouse, the City column moves to the first position.

TROUBLESHOOTING: When you begin to drag while located in a record, Access assumes that you want to change the height of the row until you move out of the column. While the mouse is inside the selected cell a black boundary forms across the entire row. Keep dragging left. As soon as the mouse moves outside the original boundaries, the gold line will appear.

b. Click any record in the **Last Name** column to select it. Move the mouse to the middle of the selected column. When the pointer shape changes to a *four-headed arrow*, click and drag right. Continue the drag until the vertical gold line is on the right edge of the report. Release the mouse.

The Last Name column is the last column in the report.

c. Click the report title, *Your Name Revenue*, to select it and then click it again to edit it. Type **Your Name Non–Miami Sales**.

d. Click the picture of the **report binder** to select it.

e. Click **Logo** in the Controls group on the Format tab.

The Insert Picture dialog box opens to the default folder, My Pictures, but the file you need is stored in the folder with the rest of the Access files.

f. Browse to your file storage folder; locate and open the file named *chap4_ho1-3_coffee.gif*. Click **OK**.

g. Move your mouse over the lower right corner of the picture until the pointer shape changes to a diagonal, double-headed arrow. Click and drag the lower-right picture corner until the picture's size roughly doubles.

The picture enlarges, but now it covers part of your name.

TIP Use the Properties Sheet to Exactly Size an Object

If you right-click the picture and select Properties from the shortcut menu, you may use measurements to exactly size the picture. You also may add special effects, like stretch or zoom.

---

h. Click the report's title, *Your Name Non–Miami Sales*, to select it. Position the mouse pointer in the middle of the box. When the pointer shape changes to the four-headed move arrow, click and drag the report title right and down (see Figure 4.11).

i. Click **Save** on the Quick Access Toolbar to save the design changes to the report.

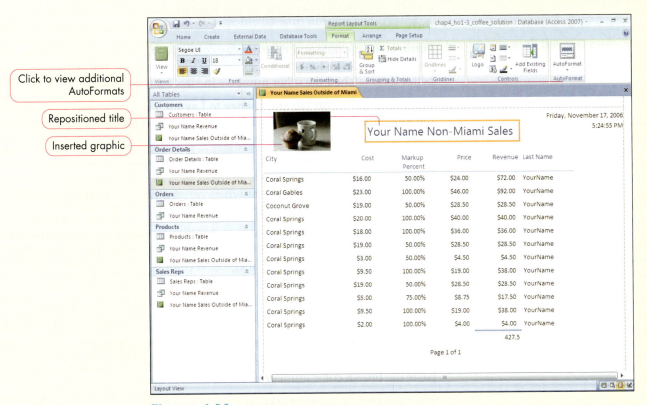

Figure 4.11   Graphic and Title Repositioned

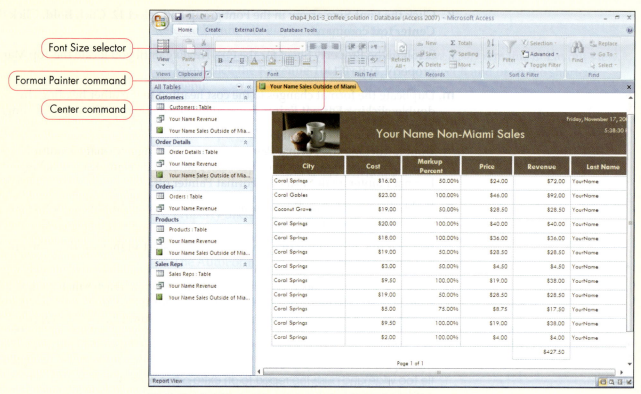

Font Size selector

Format Painter command

Center command

Figure 4.12 The Complete Single-Page Report

The Anatomy of a Report

You have produced reasonable, sophisticated output. Look at the report design depicted in Figure 4.13. It, too, contains summary statistics but on multiple levels. The desired layout contains indents to visually classify the differing elements. The finished report will likely require several pages. It would be much easier to read if the headings repeated at the start of each new page. Access can accomplish all of this, and more.

In this section you will learn more about a report's sections and controls. You will also learn how to group an Access report into nested sections.

Identifying Report Elements, Sections, and Controls

Access divides all reports into sections, although you only see the sectional boundaries when you display the report in Design view. You need to become familiar with the sectional areas so that you can control report output completely. For example, if you place an instruction to add field values together in the detail section, the resulting calculation will duplicate each record's value for that field. The field in the detail section contains a single value from a single record.

Understand Sectional Divisions

The *detail section* repeats once for each record in the underlying record source.

The *report header section* prints once at the beginning of each report.

The *report footer section* prints once at the conclusion of each report.

The *group header section(s)* appear once at the start of each new grouping level in the report.

The *group footer section(s)* appear at the end of each grouping level.

The *detail section* repeats once for each record in the underlying record source. If you copied the calculation and placed it in a report header or footer, the result would display the sum of all that field's values for the entire report. The *report header section* prints once at the beginning of each report. The *report footer section* prints once at the conclusion of each report. Should you find all the stripes and little boxes confusing, you still must learn something about them to accurately produce the output you desire. You will begin by learning about the stripes—the sectional boundaries.

In Figure 4.13, each blue stripe marks the upper boundary of a report area. The top stripe denotes the upper boundary of the report header. The bottom stripe displays the top boundary of the report's footer. The gray, grid-patterned area beneath the stripes shows the space allotted to that element. Notice that the report has no space allocated to the report footer. You may change the space between areas by moving your mouse over the stripe's bottom. When the pointer shape changes to a double-headed arrow, click and drag to move the boundary. Use this method if you decide to add a footer to the report. A gray, grid-patterned work space appears as your mouse drags down. If you expand or contract the space allotment for a middle sectional boundary, the lower boundaries all move also. The *group header section(s)* appear once at the start of each new grouping level in the report. The *group footer section(s)* appear at the end of each grouping level.

You may add summary values to additional fields using the same process. Figure 4.18 shows the results of the sum of revenue and the needed setup to calculate an average of the discounts provided customers in each product category.

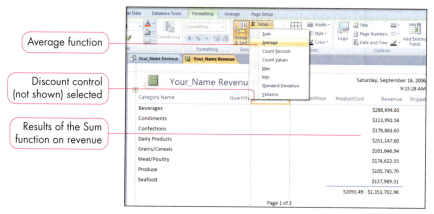

Figure 4.18 Creating an Average of the Discount Field

Add Additional Grouping Levels

You decide that having the report grouped by category is useful, but you also want to know who sells each category's products. You can add additional grouping levels to an existing report in Layout view by selecting the control that you need to group on and then clicking the Add a Group command in the Group, Sort, and Total pane. In the report displayed in Figure 4.19, you would first select the control for LastName field and then click the Add a group command. The figure displays the results of adding an additional grouping level to the report. The More command controlling the Category name group expands when selected, granting you access to additional features. The figure displays the settings necessary to display the totals (averages) for the categories below the salesperson totals.

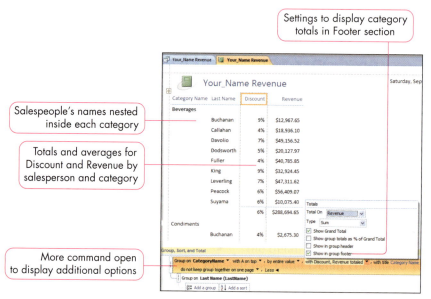

Figure 4.19 Nested Group Report with Totals Moved to Footer

Sort a Report

While working in the Layout view, you can interact with the sort order of the report's fields. Figure 4.20 shows a report with two sorting levels applied. The primary sort is the area of specialization. The secondary sort is by the physician's last name. This order groups the cardiologists together with Clark preceding Davis in the alphabetical listing.

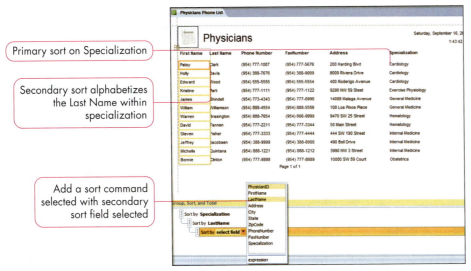

Figure 4.20 Sorted Report

Adding Fields to a Report

It is possible to omit a necessary field when designing a report. Even if a report has no errors, data needs change with time. You may need to add a new field to an existing report. Access provides an easy way to do that.

Open the report in Layout view. Activate the Format tab. Click Add Existing Fields in the Controls group. The Field List pane opens on the right side of the screen. The *Field List pane* displays a list of all of the tables and fields in the database. Once you locate the needed field in the Field List pane, drag and drop it on the report in the position that you want it to occupy. (Alternatively, you can double-click it.) Access creates the needed control to hold the new field, for example, a text box, and then binds the field to the newly created control (see Figure 4.21). Occasionally, you might

The **Field List pane** displays a list of all of the tables and fields in the database.

want a different control type than the one Access creates for you. You may edit the newly created control's properties to get exactly the control you want. But, you cannot use Layout view to do so. You cannot change the control type property in Layout view. This change must be accomplished in Design view. Of course, you may only specify a control that is appropriate to that data type. For example, a Yes/No field might display as a check box, but you would rather have the words, Yes or No, display.

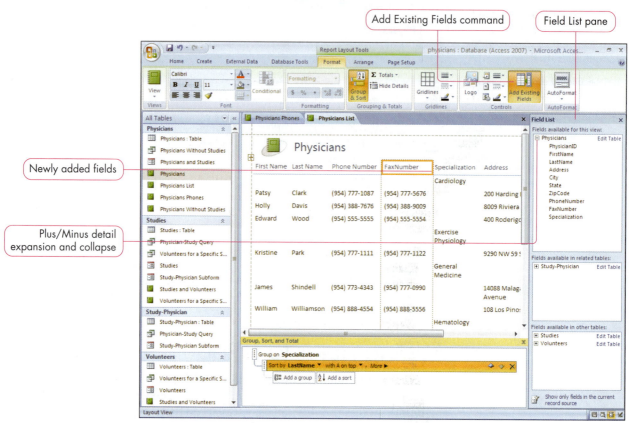

Figure 4.21 Sorted Report

In the next hands-on exercise, you will create a report, add sorting and grouping to refine the content, work with data aggregates, and add a new field to the report.

Hands-On Exercises

2 | Create, Sort, Edit, Nest, and Remove Groups from Reports

Skills covered: 1. Sort a Report **2.** Create a Grouped Report and Sort It. **3.** Add Additional Grouping Levels and Calculate Summary Statistics **4.** Remove Grouping Levels **5.** Reorder Grouping Levels

Step 1
Sort a Report

Refer to Figure 4.22 as you complete Step 1.

a. Open the *chap4_ho1-3_coffee_solution* file if necessary, click **Options** on the Security Warning toolbar, click the **Enable this content option** in the Microsoft Office Security Options dialog box, and click **OK**.

> **TROUBLESHOOTING:** If you create unrecoverable errors while completing this hands-on exercise, you can delete the *chap4_ho1-3_coffee_solution* file, copy the *chap4_ho1_coffee_solution* backup database you created at the end of the first hands-on exercise, and open the copy of the backup database to start the second hands-on exercise again.

b. Open the **Your Name Revenue query** in Datasheet view. Click the **Create tab** and click **Report**.

c. Click **Group & Sort** in the Grouping & Totals group to turn on the Group, Sort, and Total pane at the bottom of the screen.

> **TROUBLESHOOTING:** The Group & Sort command is a toggle. If you do not see the Group, Sort, and Total pane, click the Group & Sort command again. It may have been on, and you turned it off.

d. Click **Add a sort** in the Group, Sort, and Total pane.

A list box opens displaying the names of all the reports fields.

e. Click **LastName** from the list and select it.

Scroll through the list to see two names: Lockley and your name. If your name comes before Lockley alphabetically, your sales are reported first. If your name comes after Lockley alphabetically, Lockley's sales will be first. In the next step, you will sort the list so that your name is on the top—ascending or descending, depending on what letter your name begins with.

f. Find the **Sort with A on top drop-down arrow** in the Group, Sort, and Total pane. Click it to reveal two choices—with A on top and with Z on top. Click the choice that will position your name at the top of the list.

If your name is not on top, sort again, and select the other option.

g. Click the **Office Button**, choose **Save As**, and type **Sales by Employee and City**. Click **OK**.

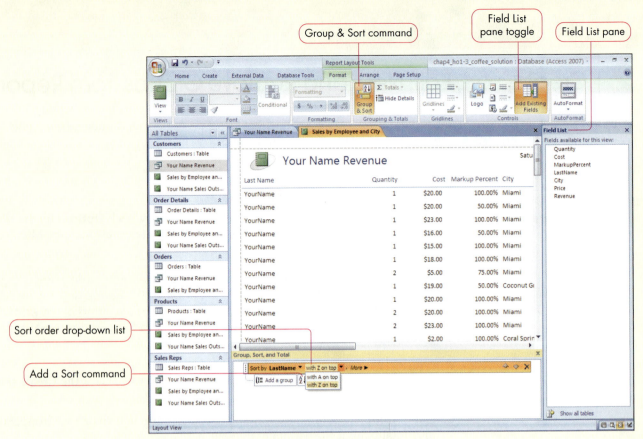

Figure 4.22 Correctly Sorted Report

<table>
<tr><td rowspan="2">

Step 2

Create a Grouped Report and Sort It

</td><td>

Refer to Figure 4.23 as you complete Step 2.

a. Click **Add a group** in the Group, Sort, and Total pane.

A list box pops up asking you to select the field name that you want to group by.

b. Select the **LastName** field in the list box.

TROUBLESHOOTING: If your screen does not look like Figure 4.23, it may be because you selected a different group by value. Click close on the gold Group on LastName bar in the Group, Sort, and Total pane to remove the incorrect grouping. Then rework Steps 2a and 2b.

c. Scroll right until you can see the label control box for the **Revenue** field. (It is blue.) Click to select it.

d. Click the **Format tab** and click **Totals** in the Grouping & Totals group.

A drop-down list providing function options appears.

e. Click **Sum**.

f. Save the report.

A sum has been added to the Revenue field after each group. You probably cannot see it because it is scrolled off-screen. Use the scrollbar to see that your revenue is 1599.125.

</td></tr>
</table>

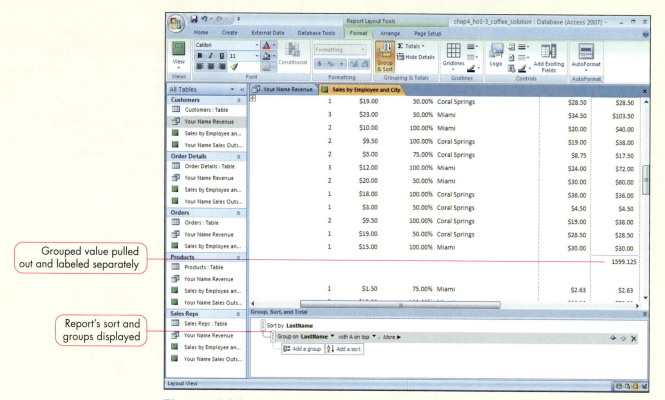

Figure 4.23 Correctly Sorted Report with Primary Group

Annotations on figure:
- Grouped value pulled out and labeled separately
- Report's sort and groups displayed

Step 3
Add Additional Grouping Levels and Calculate Summary Statistics

Refer to Figure 4.24 as you complete Step 3.

a. Ensure that you are still in Layout view. Click **Add a group** in the Group, Sort, and Total pane.

b. Scroll left to locate and select the **City** field in the Field List box.

The Primary grouping level is still the salesperson's last name. Now the customer's city is grouped together nested inside the LastName field. During this period, you sold one order to a customer in Coconut Grove, once to a customer in Coral Gables, 10 orders to customers in Coral Springs, and the rest of your orders came from Miami-based customers. You decide to create summary statistics by city and salesperson to analyze the sales information.

c. Click the **Cost** label to select it. Click **Totals** in the Grouping & Totals group. Select **Average** from the function list.

Scroll down until you see the average cost for the orders to Coral Springs displayed. You will see the average cost of an order from a Coral Springs customer was only $12.10, while the average costs of orders to Coral Gables and Coconut Grove were much higher.

d. Scroll up and click the **City** label to select it. Click **Totals** in the Grouping & Totals group. Select **Count Records** from the function list.

The City field is defined as a text field. Access presents different functions depending on whether the field contains text or numbers.

TIP Counting Records

If you create a report in Layout view and need to count the number of records, be sure to select a field that contains a non-null value for each record. If a report contained 20 records and you instructed Access to count a field that contained two null values, the resulting count would display 18. The missing values would not be included in the count. An easy way to fix this situation is to count only fields that have their Required property set to Yes. Alternatively, you can edit the field's control property. Select the text box containing the Count value, right-click, and select Properties. Click the Data tab. In the Control Source box, select and delete the expression and type =count(*).

e. Scroll to the last of the records from your customers (that is just above the name of the other salesperson, Lockley).

You see the number of records of orders sold by you—39.

f. Press **Ctrl+Home** to return to the top of the report. Select the **Markup Percent** label. Click **Totals** in the Grouping & Totals group. Select **Average** from the function list.

g. Scroll to the right. Select the **Price** label. Click the **Totals** command in the Grouping & Totals group. Select **Average** from the function list. Format as currency.

Like the Cost field, the Price field records a per-unit cost, so it does not make sense to sum it.

h. Scroll to the right. Select the **Revenue** label. Click **Totals** in the Grouping & Totals group. Select **Sum** from the function list. Check to make sure the value is formatted as currency.

TROUBLESHOOTING: A group summary statistic should automatically inherit its formatting properties from the field's format. Occasionally the group total or average calculates correctly, but it is incorrectly formatted. To correct the format, right-click the incorrectly formatted value in the Layout view of the report and select Properties from the shortcut menu. Set the Format property to the correct value, e.g., currency, and close the Property Sheet. This action forces a format correction.

i. Narrow the first two columns so that the report fits on one page horizontally. Refer to Hands-On Exercise 1, Step 3e, if you do not remember how to do this step.

j. Save the report.

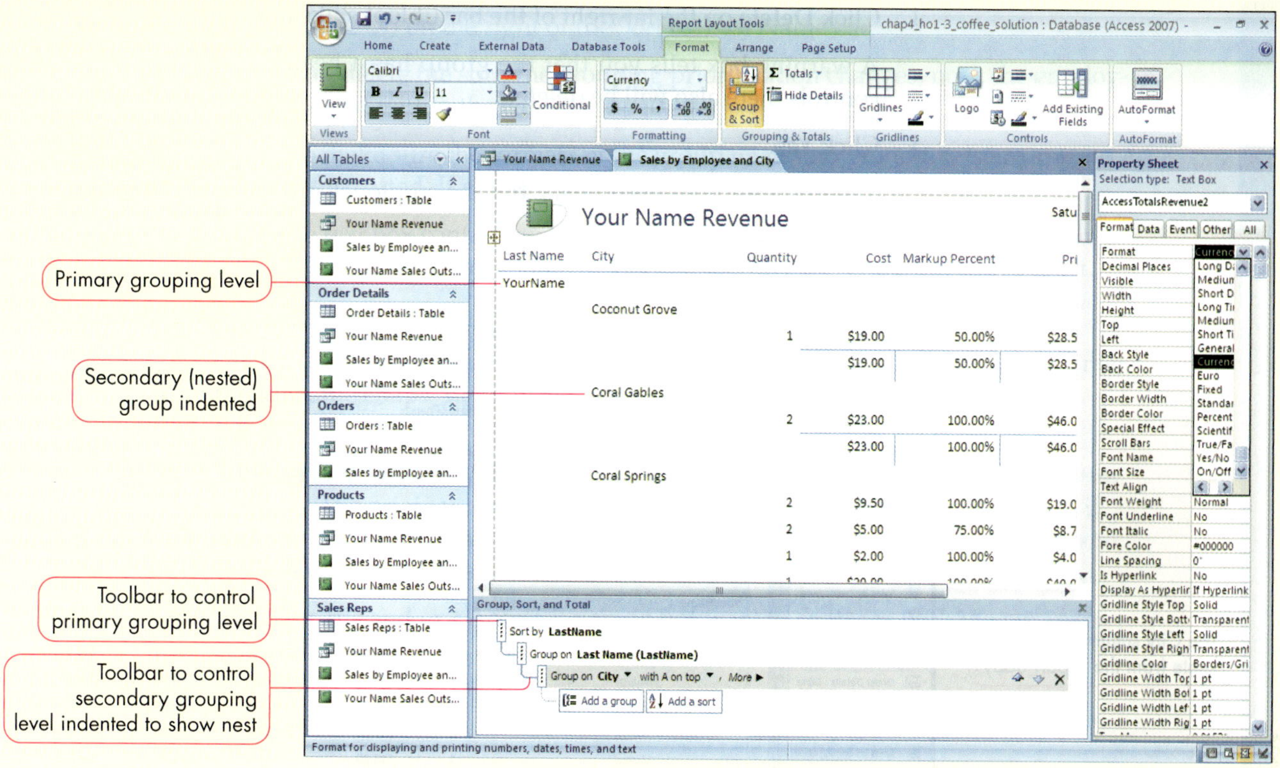

Figure 4.24 Report with Two Grouping Levels Added

Step 4
Remove Grouping Levels

Refer to Figure 4.25 as you complete Step 4.

a. Save and close the Sales by Employee and City report.

You need practice deleting grouping levels, but you need to preserve the work from Step 3. You will copy the report and delete the group levels in the copy.

b. Right-click the **Sales by Employee and City report** in the All Tables pane. Select **Copy** from the shortcut menu. Move your mouse to a white space in the All Tables pane, right-click, and select **Paste**.

c. Name the copy **Sales by Employee**. Click **OK**.

d. Move your mouse to a white space in the All Tables pane. (Do this a second time.) Right-click and select **Paste**.

e. Name the copy **Sales by City**.

TROUBLESHOOTING: If your monitor resolution is set low, you may have trouble finding white space in which to paste. This file was set to display tables and related objects in the All Tables pane. That view repeats multi-table query and report names. A view that uses less space is the Objects view. Click the All Tables pane title bar and select Object Type. That should free up some white space for you to paste the copied report. After your copied report is pasted and renamed, switch back to the Tables and related view.

f. Open the **Sales by Employee report** in Layout view.

g. Click **Group & Sort** in the Grouping & Totals group on the Format tab to display the Group, Sort, and Total pane (if necessary).

h. Click the **Group on City bar** to select it.

The entire bar turns gold when selected.

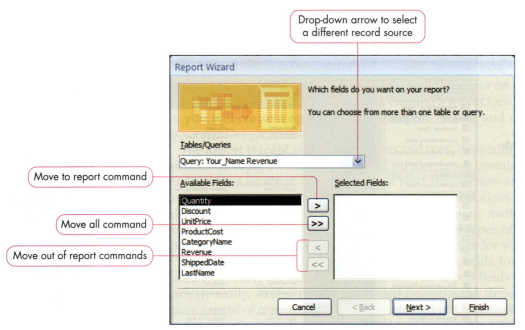

Drop-down arrow to select a different record source

Move to report command

Move all command

Move out of report commands

Figure 4.29 Select Records

Group Records

Grouping lets you organize and consolidate your data. You also can calculate aggregating information. In this report you need the data grouped by the Category Name field, so in the wizard's box under "Do you want to add any grouping levels?" you would identify and double-click the Category Name field. If you needed additional grouping levels, you would double-click those field names also. The order in which you select the groups dictates the order of nesting in the report (see Figure 4.30). The Priority commands let you change your mind and restructure the nest levels. If you select a date/time field to group by, click Grouping Options to find an interval specification box. Use it to designate the grouping interval, such as week, month, or quarter.

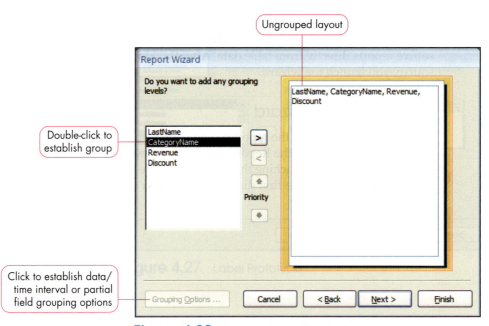

Ungrouped layout

Double-click to establish group

Click to establish data/ time interval or partial field grouping options

Figure 4.30 Specify Grouping Options

Figure 4.31 shows the grouping options set to group on Category Name. Once the group is established, the Grouping Options command activates. If the group field was a date/time field, you would establish the interval in the Grouping Intervals dialog box. Because this grouping field is a text field, the intervals displayed contain portions of the field name, i.e. the first two letters. You might use this feature if you were grouping an inventory list and the inventory IDs within a category started with the same letters. For example, FJW123, FJR123, FJB123 might be inventory numbers for the fine jewelry department for watches, rings, and bracelets. If you set the grouping interval option to the two initial letters, you would include the fine jewelry department's entire inventory.

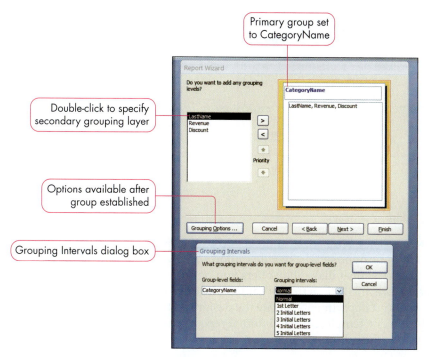

Figure 4.31 Grouping Options Set on Category

Add Sorts and Summary Instructions

The next dialog box asks "What sort order and summary information do you want for detail records?" Notice that the sorts apply only to a detail record. Some reports omit the detail, making the sort order moot. If this were a detail report, you might specify that the details be sorted first by category in ascending order and then by revenue in descending order. Because you have decided to create a summary report, you need to click the Summary Options command. This step takes you to a screen where you may choose summary statistics (sum, average, minimum, and maximum), and whether or not you want the details presented (see Figure 4.32). Clicking either OK or Cancel returns you to the wizard.

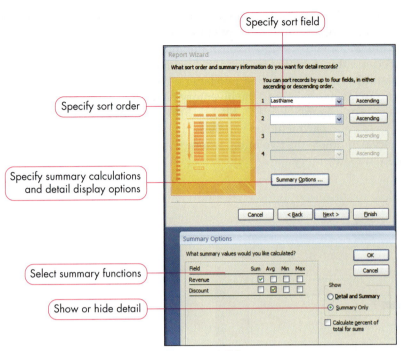

Specify sort field

Specify sort order

Specify summary calculations and detail display options

Select summary functions

Show or hide detail

Figure 4.32 Specify Sort Options

Design the Report

The next two dialog boxes control the report's appearance. In the first you select the layout from three options. Clicking an option will give you a general preview in the preview area. The final dialog box offers you options among the AutoFormats available (see Figure 4.33). In actual organizations, the Public Relations and Graphic Communications departments dictate the design of all printed output. The organization will have one template for all internal reports and one or two others for reports generated for external consumption (e.g., an invoice).

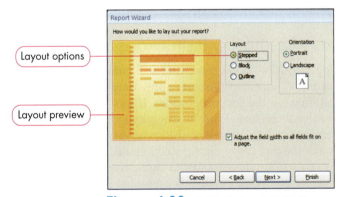

Layout options

Layout preview

Figure 4.33 Specify Layout Options

A **work-around** acknowledges that a problem exists, and develops a sufficing solution.

Ironically, the design selection variety makes life more difficult for students than for real-world practitioners. On the job, you typically employ fewer than five templates. You use them all day, every day. You become intimately acquainted with all of their quirks. You develop functional work-arounds. A **work-around** acknowledges that a problem exists and develops a sufficing solution. In a course, you use a variety of differing templates and never fully understand any of them. Figure 4.34 shows AutoFormat choices.

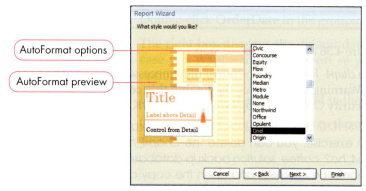

Figure 4.34 AutoFormat

Save and Name the Report

A well-designed database may contain only a few tables, but it may have many queries and reports. You should name all report objects descriptively to save you time and minimize frustration. Always name your report something that not only makes sense to you today, but also will communicate the report's contents to a co-worker or to you in six months (see Figure 4.35).

In the next hands-on exercise you will create a report using the Report Wizard and edit it using the Layout view.

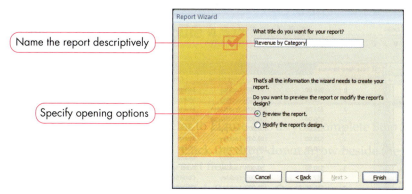

Figure 4.35 Use Descriptive Report Names

13. What happens if you click a value in Layout view and press Delete?

    (a) The entire column is deleted from the report, and column widths are adjusted to use the empty space.

    (b) Nothing; you cannot change data in Layout view.

    (c) The record is deleted from the report but remains in the database.

    (d) An error message appears, saying that you should not attempt to manipulate records in a report.

14. Your pointer shape should be a _____ to widen or narrow a column in Layout view.

    (a) single arrow

    (b) hand

    (c) two-headed arrow

    (d) dashed-tail arrow

15. Which of these is not a sectional division used in Access?

    (a) Detail section

    (b) Report header and footer sections

    (c) Group header and footer sections

    (d) Summary section

16. Bound controls are so called because they are bound or attached to:

    (I) source data

    (II) the report's margins

    (a) I but not II

    (b) II but not I

    (c) Both I and II

    (d) Neither I nor II

17. Which of the following is true?

    (a) Unbound controls are used infrequently within reports.

    (b) Unbound controls are used to display cosmetic elements in a report.

    (c) Unbound controls must be saved separately because they are not part of a record.

    (d) Unbound controls cannot be used with bound controls in the same report.

18. To organize your data in a highly usable and readable report, you may use:

    (a) Nested tables

    (b) Nested groups

    (c) Nested queries

    (d) Calculated fields

Practice Exercises

1 Comfort Insurance Raises and Bonuses Report

The Comfort Insurance Agency is a midsized company with offices located across the country. The Human Resource office is located in the home office in Miami. Each year, each employee receives a performance review. The review determines employee eligibility for salary increases and the annual performance bonus. The employee data are stored in an Access database, which is used by the Human Resource department to monitor and maintain employee records. Your task is to prepare a report showing the salary increase for each employee and his or her performance bonuses (if any). You are the Human Resource department manager. If you correctly report the employee salaries and bonuses, you will receive a bonus. Work carefully and check the accuracy of the calculations. This project follows the same set of skills as used in Hands-On Exercises 1 and 2 in this chapter. If you have problems, reread the detailed directions presented in the chapter. Compare your results to Figure 4.41.

a. Copy the partially completed file *chap4_pe1_insurance* to your production folder. Rename it **chap4_pe1_insurance_solution**, open the file, and enable the security content.

b. Click the **Database Tools tab** and click **Relationships** in the Show/Hide group. Examine the table structure, relationships, and fields. After you are familiar with the database, close the Relationships window.

c. Rename the query with **your name**. Open the **Your Name Raises and Bonus query**.

d. Click the **Create tab** and click **Report** in the Reports group.

e. Click **Group & Sort** in the Grouping & Totals group, if necessary. Click **Add a sort** in the Group, Sort, and Total pane and select **LastName**.

f. Click the **LastName** label. Click it again to edit it and add a **space** between *Last* and *Name*. Click outside the text box to turn off editing. Move the mouse to the **right** control boundary, and when the pointer shape changes to the double-headed arrow click and drag the boundary about a half-inch to the left to make the column narrower.

g. Repeat Step f to add a space to the *FirstName* control and decrease its width. Also reduce the width for the *Performance* column. The report should only be one page wide. Add spaces to the *2008Increase* and *NewSalary* controls.

h. Click the **Report Graphic** (the picture in the upper left) to select it. Click **Logo** in the Controls group on the Format tab. Browse to and locate the file named *chap4_pe1_confident.jpg*. Click **OK** in the Insert Picture dialog box.

i. Click the report title *Your Name Raises and Bonuses* to select it. Point the mouse at the middle of the control box and when the pointer shape changes to the four-headed, move arrow, move the report title right.

j. Click the **Confidential graphic** and drag the **right** boundary right to enlarge the warning.

k. Right-click any number in the **New Salary** field and select **Properties** from the shortcut menu. Set the Format property in the Property Sheet to **Currency** and close the Property Sheet.

l. Right-click any number in the **Bonus** field and select **Properties**. Set the **Format property** to **Currency**. Close the Property Sheet.

m. Right-click the report tab and switch to **Print Preview**. If your report looks like the one in the figure, save the report as **Your Name Raises and Bonuses**.

n. Close the database.

...continued on Next Page

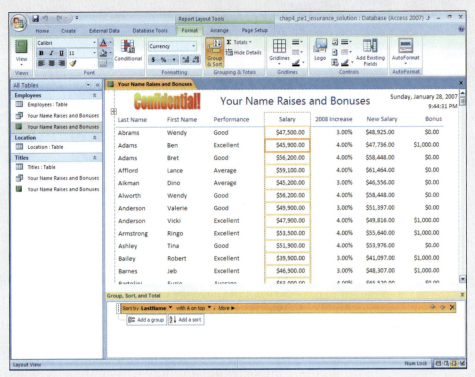

Figure 4.41 Raises and Bonuses Report

2 Comfort Insurance Raises by Location

The Comfort Insurance Agency is a midsized company with offices located across the country. The Human Resource office is located in the home office in Miami. Each year, each employee receives a performance review. The review determines employee eligibility for salary increases and the annual performance bonus. The employee data are stored in an Access database. This database is used by the Human Resource department to monitor and maintain employee records. Your task is to prepare a report showing employee raises and bonuses by city. You will need to total the payroll and bonus data for each city. You are the Human Resource department manager. If you correctly prepare the report, you will receive a bonus. This project follows the same set of skills as used in Hands-On Exercises 1 and 2 in this chapter. If you have problems, reread the detailed directions presented in the chapter. Compare your results to Figure 4.42.

a. Copy the partially completed file *chap4_pe2_insurance.accdb* to your production folder. Rename it **chap4_pe2_insurance_solution.accdb**, open the copied file, and enable the security content.

b. Click the **Database Tools tab** and click **Relationships** in the Show/Hide group. Examine the table structure, relationships, and fields. After you are familiar with the database, close the Relationships window.

c. Open the **Employees Query** in Datasheet view. Click the **Create tab** and click **Report** in the Reports group.

d. Click **Add Existing Fields** in the Controls group on the Format tab. The Field List pane opens on the right. In the bottom of the Field List pane is the *Fields available in related tables pane*. Click the **Show all tables** link. The Location table is listed with a plus sign next to it. Click the **plus sign** to reveal the hidden fields available in the Location table.

e. Double-click the **Location** field (not the LocationID field) to add it to the report. Because this field is in a table not in the original record source Access asks if it is OK to create a new query that contains the Location field. Click **Yes**. The city names add to the report. The new field is selected. Close the Field List pane.

f. Click the **Location** text box at the top of the field. Move the mouse to the middle of the selected Location field and when the mouse pointer assumes the four-headed move shape, click and drag the field to the **leftmost** position in the report.

...continued on Next Page

g. Click the **LastName** text box at the top of the field to select it. Click it a second time to edit it. Type a **space** between Last and Name. Add spaces to **FirstName**, **HireDate**, **2008Increase**, **2008Raise**, **YearHired**, and **YearsWorked**.

h. Select the **Last Name** field. Move the mouse pointer over the right boundary and when the pointer shape changes to a double-headed arrow, click and drag **left** to narrow the column. Repeat this step for the **First Name** field.

i. Right-click any record in the **2008 Raise** field and select **Properties**. In the Properties Sheet, set the Format property to **Currency**. Close the Property Sheet.

j. Select the **Year Hired** field and delete it. Adjust any field column widths as necessary to make sure all the columns fit on one page.

k. Click **Group & Sort** in the Grouping & Totals group to turn on the Group, Sort, and Total pane (if necessary). Click **Add a group** in the Group, Sort, and Total pane. Click **Location** in the Group on Select field box.

l. Click the **More Options** command on the Group on Location bar. Click the drop-down arrow beside "with LastName totaled." Click the drop-down arrow in the Total On box and select **2008Raise**. Click the **Show Grand Total** and **Show in group footer** check boxes. Click anywhere outside the Total by box.

m. Click the report title and change it to **Your Name**.

n. Click the **Office Button**. Position the mouse pointer over **Print** and click **Print Preview**. Print the report.

o. Save the report as **Your Name Raises by Location**. Close the database.

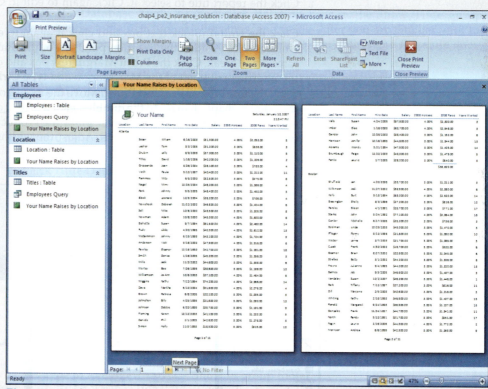

Figure 4.42   Raises by Location Shown in Print Preview

3 Northwind Traders

Northwind Traders is a small, international, specialty food company. It sells products in eight different divisions: beverages, confections (candy), condiments, dairy products, grains and cereals, meat and poultry, produce, and seafood. Although most of its customers are restaurants and gourmet food shops, it has a few retail customers, too. The firm purchases merchandise from a variety of suppliers. All of the order and inventory information is stored in the company's database. This database is used by the management to monitor and maintain records. You are the marketing manager. Your task is to prepare a report showing the profitability of the products in your inventory. You need to group the products by their categories. You also need to average the profit

...continued on Next Page

Duplex printer A printing device that prints on both sides of the page.

Expression A formula used to calculate new fields from the values in existing fields.

Expression Builder A tool to help you create a formula that performs calculations easily.

Field A basic entity, data element, or category, such as a book title or telephone number.

Field List pane Displays a list of all of the tables and fields in the database.

Field size property Defines how much space to reserve for each field.

Filter Condition that helps you find a subset of data meeting your specifications.

Filter by Form Permits selecting the criteria from a drop-down list, or applying multiple criterion.

Filter by Selection Selects only the records that match the pre-selected criteria.

Find Locates a word or group of words in a file.

Flat or non-relational Data contained in a single page or sheet (not multiple).

Font A complete set of characters—upper- and lowercase letters, numbers, punctuation marks, and special symbols with the same design.

Foreign key A field in one table that also is stored in a different table as a primary key.

Form An interface that enables you to enter or modify record data.

Format Painter Feature that enables you to copy existing text formats to other text to ensure consistency.

Formatting text Changes an individual letter, a word, or a body of selected text.

Front end Contains the objects, like queries, reports and forms, needed to interact with data, but not the tables where the record values reside.

Gallery Displays a set of predefined options that can be clicked to apply to an object or to text.

Go To Moves the insertion point to a specific location in the file.

Group Categories that organize similar commands together within each tab on the Ribbon.

Group footer section(s) Appear at the end of each grouping level.

Group header section(s) Appear once at the start of each new grouping level in the report.

IIF function The function that evaluates a condition and executes one action when the condition is true and an alternate action when the condition is false.

Indexed property A list that relates the field values to the records that contain the field value.

Inequity Examines a mathematical relationship such as equals, not equals, greater than, less than, greater than or equal to, or less than or equal to.

Insert The process of adding text in a document, spreadsheet cell, database object, or presentation slide.

Insertion point The blinking vertical line in the document, cell, slide show, or database table designating the current location where text you type displays.

Key Tip The letter or number that displays over each feature on the Ribbon and Quick Access Toolbar and is the keyboard equivalent that you press. Press Alt by itself to display Key Tips.

Label Wizard Asks you questions and then, depending on how you answer, generates the report formatted to print on mailing labels.

Landscape orientation Page orientation is wider than it is long, resembling a landscape scene.

Layout view Alter the report design while viewing the data.

Live Preview A feature that provides a preview of how a gallery option will affect the current text or object when the mouse pointer hovers over the gallery option.

Macro Small program that automates tasks in a file.

Mailing labels Self-stick, die-cut labels that you print with names, addresses, and postal barcodes.

Manual duplex Operation that enables you to print on both sides of the paper by printing first on one side and then on the other.

Mini toolbar A semitransparent toolbar of often-used font, indent, and bullet commands that displays when you position the mouse over selected text and disappears when you move the mouse away from the selected text.

Nested groups Provide a power-layering tool to organize information.

Not operator Returns the opposite of the specified criteria.

Null The formal, computer term for a missing value.

Object An entity that contains the basic elements of the database. Access uses six types of objects—tables, queries, forms, reports, macros, and modules.

Office Button Icon that, when clicked, displays the Office menu.

Office menu List of commands (such as New, Open, Save, Save As, Print, and Options) that work with an entire file or with the specific Microsoft Office program.

One-to-many relationship Exists when each record in the first table may match one, more than one, or no records in the second table. Each record in the second table matches one and only one record in the first table.

Operand Field or value being operated or manipulated in an expression.

Or operator Returns records meeting any of the specified criteria.

Order of precedence Rules that establish the sequence by which values are calculated.

Overtype mode Replaces the existing text with text you type character by character.

Page footers Appear once for each page in the report at the bottom of the pages.

Page headers Appear once for each page in the report at the top of the pages.

Paste Places the cut or copied text or object in the new location.

PivotChart view Displays a chart of the associated PivotTable view.

PivotTable view Provides a convenient way to summarize and organize data about groups of records.

PMT function Calculates a periodic loan payment given a constant interest rate, term, and original value.

PNPI Federal laws governing the safeguarding of personal, non-public information such as Social Security numbers (SSNs), credit card or bank account numbers, medical or educational records, or other sensitive data.

Portrait orientation Page orientation is longer than it is wide—like the portrait of a person.

Presentation graphics software A computer application, such as Microsoft PowerPoint, that is used primarily to create electronic slide shows.

Primary key The field that makes each record in a table unique.

Print Preview view Displays the report as it will be printed.

Property A characteristic or attribute of an object that determines how the object looks and behaves.

Query A database object that enables you to ask questions about the data stored in a database and returns the answers in the order from the records that match your instructions.

Query design grid Displays when you select a query's Design view; it divides the window into two parts.

Query sort order Determines the order of items in the query datasheet view.

Query Wizard A tool that facilitates new query development.

Quick Access Toolbar A customizable row of buttons for frequently used commands, such as Save and Undo.

Record A complete set of all of the data (fields) about one person, place, event, or idea.

Redo Command that reinstates or reserves an action performed by the Undo command.

Referential Integrity The set of rules that ensure that data stored in related tables remain consistent as the data are updated.

Relational Database Management System Data are grouped into similar collections, called tables, and the relationships between tables are formed by using a common field.

Relational database software A computer application, such as Microsoft Access, that is used to store data and convert it into information.

Replace The process of finding and replacing a word or group of words with other text.

Report A printed document that displays information professionally from a database.

Report footer section Prints once at the conclusion of each report.

Report header section Prints once at the beginning of each report.

Report view Provides you the ability to see what the printed report will look like and to make temporary changes to how the data are viewed.

Report Wizard Asks you questions and then, depending on how you answer, generates the report.

Ribbon The Microsoft Office 2007 GUI command center that organizes commands into related tabs and groups.

Run a query Processes the query instructions and displays records that meet the conditions.

Sarbanes Oxley Act (SOX) Protects the general public and companies' shareholders against fraudulent practices and accounting errors.

Select query Searches the underlying tables to retrieve the data that satisfy the query parameters.

Shortcut menu A list of commands that appears when you right-click an item or screen element.

Sort Lists those records in a specific sequence, such as alphabetically by last name or rearranges data based on a certain criteria.

Sort Ascending Provides an alphabetical list of text data or a small-to-large list of numeric data.

Sort Descending Arranges the records with the highest value listed first.

Spreadsheet program A computer application, such as Microsoft Excel, that is used to build and manipulate electronic spreadsheets.

Status bar The horizontal bar at the bottom of a Microsoft Office application that displays summary information about the selected window or object and contains View buttons and the Zoom slider. The Word status bar displays the page number and total words, while the Excel status bar displays the average, count, and sum of values in a selected range. The PowerPoint status bar displays the slide number and the Design Theme name.

Syntax The set of rules by which the words and symbols of an expression are correctly combined.

Tab Looks like a folder tab and divides the Ribbon into task-oriented categories.

Table A collection of records. Every record in a table contains the same fields in the same order.

Table row The second row of the query design grid that specifies the tables from which the fields are selected to create a query.

Template A file that incorporates a theme, a layout, and content that can be modified.

Title bar The shaded bar at the top of every window; often displays the program name and filename.

Total row Displays as the last row in the Datasheet view of a table or query and provides a variety of summary statistics.

Totals query Organizes query results into groups by including a grouping field and a numeric field for aggregate calculations.

Unbound controls Do not have any record source for their contents.

Undo Command cancels your last one or more operations.

User interface The meeting point between computer software and the person using it.

Validation rule Checks the authenticity of the data entered in a field.

Virus checker Software that scans files for a hidden program that can damage your computer.

Word processing software A computer application, such as Microsoft Word, that is used primarily with text to create, edit, and format documents.

Work-around Acknowledges that a problem exists, and develops a sufficing solution.

Zoom slider Enables you to increase or decrease the magnification of the file onscreen.

Multiple Choice Answer Keys

Office Fundamentals, Chapter 1

1. b
2. c
3. d
4. a
5. d
6. c
7. b
8. c
9. d
10. a
11. c
12. d
13. c
14. a
15. d

Access 2007, Chapter 1

1. b
2. b
3. d
4. d
5. b
6. b
7. b
8. c
9. c
10. c
11. c
12. a
13. c
14. d
15. a

Access 2007, Chapter 2

1. b
2. c
3. b
4. a
5. d
6. b
7. d
8. c
9. b
10. b
11. d
12. d
13. b
14. c
15. c
16. b
17. c
18. b
19. d
20. b

Access 2007, Chapter 3

1. a
2. c
3. e
4. d
5. b
6. c
7. a
8. a
9. a
10. c
11. a
12. b
13. b
14. c
15. d

Access 2007, Chapter 4

1. b
2. d
3. d
4. c
5. c
6. b
7. d
8. c
9. b
10. d
11. a
12. c
13. a
14. c
15. d
16. a
17. b
18. b

Index

P

Page footer section, 272, 273, 299
Page header section, 272, 273, 299
Page Orientation command, 25
Paste command, 35, 53
Paste Options button, 34
Payment (PMT) function, 214–215
  arguments for, 215
  exercise with, 224–226, 246–247
Pencil symbol, 75
Personal, non-public information
  (PNPI), 134
  database design and safeguarding
  of, 134
Phishing document exercise, 58–59
PivotChart view, 139
PivotTable view, 139
Plagiarism, 43
PMT function. *See* Payment function
PNPI. *See* Personal, non-public
  information
Portrait orientation, 25
PowerPoint 2007, Microsoft, 3
  file formats for, 23
  help in dialog box and, 12
  Office Button in, 12
  presentation graphics software and, 3
  Ribbon in, 7
  Zoom slider and, 12
Presentation graphics software, 3
  characteristics of, 3
  PowerPoint as, 3
Prestige Hotel chain exercise, 195–196
  member rewards in, 243–244,
    307–308
Primary keys, 75, 89, 95, 102, 111,
  138, 139
  changing of, 144
  data sharing and designation of, 153
Print dialog box, 26, 30
  print options in, 26
Print Preview, 25–26, 60
  Access and, 57
  exercise with, 29
  report in, 257–258, 299
Print Preview tab, 25
Print Preview Window, 25, 60
Printers, duplex, 27
Printing
  both sides of paper and, 27
  files and, 18, 24–27, 30, 53, 59–60
  options for, 26
  preview of file before, 25–26, 60
  Quick Print feature and, 27
Production folder
  creation of, 81–82
Promotion flyer exercise, 60–61
Properties
  Allow Zero Length, 141
  Caption, 140, 141, 145
  Default Value, 141
  definition of, 140

  description of, 141
  Field, 145–148
  Field Size, 133, 141, 145, 146
  Format, 141, 162
  IME Mode, 141
  IME Sentence Mode, 141
  Indexed, 141, 150
  Input Mask, 141
  reference list for, 141
  Required, 141
  smart tags and, 141
  Unicode Compression, 141
  Validation Rule, 141
  Validation Text, 141
Protection
  databases and data, 87, 165
  referential integrity and
    data, 165

Q

Queries, 76–77, 111, 166
  calculated fields in, 203–206
  coffee revenue, 127, 251
  copying of, 173, 183
  creation of, 166–168, 183, 194–195
  criteria for, 168
  definition of, 77, 166
  detailed, 176
  examining record number in, 167
  exercise with multiple-table,
    178–182
  filters *v.*, 168
  large database, 177, 183
  multiple choice test for, 237–238
  naming of, 176
  National Bank, 310–311
  Null criteria expressions in, 170, 171
  operands in, 169–170
  reordering of fields in, 171
  running of, 173, 183
  saving of, 205
  select, 167
  summary, 176
  total row in, 229
  Totals, 229–230, 236
Query Datasheet View, 168
Query design grid, 166
  Criteria rows in, 168
  Field row in, 168
  panes in, 168
  Show row in, 168
  Sort row in, 168
  Table row in, 171
  use of, 168
Query Design View, 167
Query sort order, 171
Query Wizard, 166, 183
  detailed/summary query selection
    in, 176
  exercise with, 178
  launching of, 174
  naming of query with, 176

  selection of Simple Query Wizard in,
    174
  Tables/Queries drop-down box in,
    174, 175
  use of, 173–176
Question mark wild cards, 169
Quick Access Toolbar, 4, 5, 53
  customizing of, 5
Quick Print feature, 27

R

RAM. *See* Memory
Real estate development report, 316
Real estate report exercise, 311–312
Real world databases, 177
Recent Documents list
  keeping files on, 21
  opening of files with, 20–21
Record Status indicator, 90
Records, 71, 111
  addition of, 85–86
  counting of, 284
  deletion of, 86–87
  editing of, 83–84
Redo button, 39
Redo command, 39, 53
Referential integrity, 102, 111, 149
  data protection and, 165
  database design and, 135, 183
Relational data, 94–95
Relational database management
  system, 102
Relational database software, 3
  Access as, 3
  characteristics of, 3
Relational databases, 102, 103–104, 111
  multiple choice test for, 185–186
  power of, 149
Relational operators, 99
Relationship view, 111
Relationships exercise, 105–110
  Filter by Form in, 107–108
  filtering of report in, 108–109
  removal of advanced filter in,
    109–110
  table data changes in, 106–107
Relationships, table, 154–158, 183
  definitions of, 155
  deletion of, 158
  editing of, 158
  establishment of, 163–164, 183
  many-to-many, 155
  one-to-many, 154, 155–158
  one-to-one, 155
  reference list of, 155
Relationships window, 102–103, 111
  design view and, 156
  exercise with, 105–106
  one-to-many relationship and, 155,
    156, 157, 158
Repair utility. *See* Compact and Repair
  utility